WHO CARES?

Other Books by Roy McConkey

LET ME SPEAK (*with Dorothy M. Jeffree*)
LET ME PLAY (*with Dorothy M. Jeffree and Simon Hewson*)
TEACHING THE HANDICAPPED CHILD (*with Dorothy M. Jeffree and Simon Hewson*)
LET'S MAKE TOYS (*with Dorothy M. Jeffree*)
BREAKING BARRIERS (*with Bob McCormack*)
LET'S TALK (*with Penny Price*)
WORKING WITH PARENTS (*Croom Helm*)

HUMAN HORIZONS SERIES

WHO CARES?

Community involvement with mental handicap

ROY McCONKEY

A CONDOR BOOK
SOUVENIR PRESS (E & A) LTD

First published 1987 by Souvenir Press
(Educational & Academic) Ltd,
43 Great Russell Street, London WC1B 3PA
and simultaneously in Canada

ISBN 0 285 65044 0 (casebound)
ISBN 0 285 65049 1 (paperback)

Photoset, printed and bound in Great Britain by
WBC Bristol and Maesteg.

For my wife Pat

Acknowledgements

My sincere thanks go to the following for their help and support:

* My colleagues in St Michael's House, especially Bob McCormack and Jodie Walsh who helped to design and execute the surveys described in the book and made valuable comments on the first draft.
* St Michael's House Research Committee who wholly funded the research programme, and to Dr Barbara Stokes, its chairperson, for her constant encouragement.
* The many friends and colleagues who gave freely of their time to help with interviewing, and to John Byrne for the cartoons.
* The people of North Dublin who took the time to answer our questions. Truly, without them, the book would not have been possible.

Contents

Preface

Community care for disabled people has been slow in becoming a reality. The promised revolution stutters along, susceptible to the vagaries of inadequate financing and disputed objectives. In retrospect, there has been an appalling omission. Little or no attempt has been made to understand the community; to identify who in the community are likely to care or to involve them in decisions about the form and style of services.

Instead:

* There has been a preoccupation with preparing disabled people for life in the community but little on preparing the community for life with the disabled.
* Professionals in services may be expert in caring for individual disabled people but few will be knowledgeable about local community networks or have the experience of coping with communities of non-disabled people. They need to broaden their expertise and experience if the new service models are to flourish.
* Community care has been promoted as a philosophy rather than as a plan of action. Consequently, even the initial fact-finding steps have yet to be taken.

Who Cares? aims to rectify this omission. Written with service providers, professional workers, concerned parents and disabled activists in mind, it critically examines the concept of community with particular reference to person-to-person services, and presents the findings of a major research study which involved more than 600 individual interviews with representative samples in suburban housing estates and shopping centres.

The book documents local people's past involvement

with disability, their perceptions of what it means to be handicapped, their preparedness to meet disabled people and their willingness to know and to do more. Throughout the book the findings are not left as bald facts and figures. Rather, the implications for action are spelt out; most challenge long-held but untested presumptions and some conflict markedly with existing practices. And, for the first time, pen-pictures are given of the people in the community who are the most likely allies in furthering community-based services.

The book was written with a second purpose in mind, namely to take the mystery out of research methodology. The rationale for procedures used and the implications for interpreting the results are spelt out through many examples. It is hoped that this object lesson will empower and encourage readers to undertake their own community research projects. Sample questionnaires are included in the Appendices.

Who Cares? completes a trilogy of publications to emerge from a research programme which examined the needs of mentally handicapped adults living in the community; their participation in community life; the involvement of local people in learning more about mental handicap and ways of involving the community in helping their mentally handicapped peers and families.

The story begun here is continued in our book, *Breaking Barriers*[1] which explores the why and how of educating people about disability; describes ready-made packages, which have been tried and tested in Ireland, and gives detailed guidelines for people wishing to prepare their own programmes of community education.

The third book, *Let's Make Friends* by Jodie Walsh,[2] describes schemes for engaging ordinary people in meeting some of the needs of disabled people and their families, primarily through person-to-person help in everyday settings and by doing everyday things.

One of the first studies in this series was undertaken by Francesca Lundström-Roche[3] with support from the Irish

Committee for the International Year of Disabled People in 1981. She interviewed 54 trainees attending sheltered workshops for mildly and moderately mentally handicapped people in Dublin. They talked about their lifestyles, their likes and dislikes and, most importantly of all, their feelings about being disabled. As a reminder that it is they, and people like them, who lie behind every page of these three books, I begin each chapter with a quotation taken from Francesca's report, *Our Lives.*

Perhaps the most poignant comment came from a young woman, well-liked by staff and co-workers, who said:

> *I'd like to go home and let everything start all over again. Start my life all over again.*

And another, from a man very interested in photography, who described his life thus:

> *It's always the same face, like only having one last snap in the camera . . . you keep looking at that one and you can remember all the other times in the past you have done this.*

Many of these people, although living in the community, had few friends or out-of-home activities to enrich their lives. It may be rather too much to hope that any one research project, aimed at linking the community with mentally handicapped people, would radically affect their lifestyles but if we have increased the likelihood of this happening in the future, we shall be happy.

1 Who Cares?

> I'd like to have outside work and more money. I'd like a bigger variety of work. It can become boring—it's the same in the outside world but there you always have a choice.
>
> *Man attending Day Centre engaged in contract work*

In a hit song of the 'sixties, Bob Dylan sang about the changing times. I doubt if he or his contemporaries gave much thought to mentally handicapped people as they dreamed their dreams of a new era, yet that was the decade in which the seeds of a new philosophy of care were sown. Out went old notions of sending these people away to institutions. The concept of community care was born.

Two decades later, the experiences of planning new styles of services for people with disabilities more than bear out John Calhoun's contention that 'the interval between the decay of the old and the formation and the establishment of the new, constitutes a period of transition which must necessarily be one of uncertainty, confusion, error and wild and fierce fanaticism.'

Perhaps Calhoun's experiences in American politics, in the years preceding the Civil War, caused him to exaggerate somewhat. Yet I wonder. In the last 20 years, services for mentally handicapped people have had their share of uncertainties, confusions, errors and indeed fanatics. Even so, a remarkable consensus has been reached internationally[4] on service policy—institutions should be run down and community services developed. Sad to say, practice is a different story.

Michael Bayley's[5] conclusions about community care are just as true today as they were 13 years ago: 'The main emphasis has been on services IN the community rather than care BY the community.' In particular he noted that no attempt had been made to interweave statutory and informal care, such as might be provided by family and neighbours.

Ten years on, the Welsh Office,[6] when instigating their 'All Wales strategy for the development of services' concluded that 'the services which are provided (currently) are in many cases inadequate; facilities are too large, too impersonal and insufficiently localised to provide for the integration of mentally handicapped people in their communities and to offer the chance to develop a variety of personal relationships.' They also noted that 'present community services . . . are piecemeal and nowhere comprehensive and fully integrated.' The Welsh experience is no different, I suspect, from others throughout these islands.[7, 8]

LESSONS FROM THE PAST

How come there is such a mismatch between the ideal and

the reality? In retrospect, four failings can be identified. The first was spotted some 25 years ago, when Richard Titmuss[9] wrote: 'What progress have we made . . . in working out the concept of community care? Beyond a few brave ventures, one cannot find much evidence of attempts to hammer out the practice, as distinct from the theory of community care for the mentally ill and subnormal.'

Likewise, David Wilkin[10] concluded, 'The failure to specify in detail and plan the development of the sorts of services necessary, has produced a practical reality which is very different from the theory. Community care has come to mean care outside of an institution, or sometimes care in special sorts of rather small institutions which are located in areas of residential housing.'

He asserts that the closest we have come to community care is leaving families single-handedly to get on with the job of looking after their handicapped son or daughter. Lesson 1, then, is:

1 THE COMMUNITY'S CONTRIBUTION MUST BE SPELT OUT

The second failure was a lack of financial commitment. Peggy Jay's'[11] Government-appointed Committee did not mince their words: 'A policy of gradualism will never achieve a decent and dignified life for mentally handicapped people; what is needed is positive action and a political commitment to a major shift in priorities for expenditure.' (p. 139)

This message may eventually have got through to the Cabinet, judging by this remark by Nicholas Edwards,[6] Secretary of State for Wales: 'We need to redouble our efforts to correct the historical anomaly . . . which has left the bulk of public service provision in large and, for many, remote hospitals whilst the great majority of mentally handicapped people and their families receive little or no support in their home where it is most needed. This inadequacy of care in the community creates a cycle of dependence on institutional care because this is often the only option open to families who can no longer cope on their own.'

Amidst the rhetoric of community care, we forgot that money talks louder than words. Lesson 2:

2 COMMUNITY CARE NEEDS ASSURED FUNDING

The third failing was highlighted by Peter Townsend[12] some 15 years ago. He noted that 'any proposed change of policy which appears to threaten the interests of bodies holding considerable power is likely to be resisted and to be diverted to those interests.' He goes on to mention specifically the opposition of the nursing and medical professions to the closure of the long-stay hospitals. But David Wilkin[10] reminds us that this is true of all professional groups. 'The content and organisation of services

is often based on professional evaluations of what is best, modified by bureaucratic considerations, what the professionals are able to offer and the power struggles that go on between different professional groups. Not only do services often fail to respond to the expressed needs of their clients, but also there is often little agreement between the professionals themselves on what services should be provided.' Lesson 3:

3 SPECIALIST STAFF ROLES HAVE TO CHANGE

The fourth lesson is arguably the most damning of all:

4 THE COMMUNITY WERE NEVER CONSULTED

Very few attempts[13] have been made at either national or local levels to deal with such fundamental issues as:

* What level of awareness is there in the community about mental handicap and what contacts are there between handicapped and non-handicapped people?

* How many people in the community express a willingness to get involved in helping?
* Who are the people most likely to want to help out and what are they interested in doing?
* What are the characteristics of mentally handicapped people living in the community, especially those over 15 years of age? What can they do/not do for themselves and what sort of lives are they leading? Is it reasonable to expect community helpers to cope?
* How can the community be educated about the needs of mentally handicapped people and helped to overcome their fears or apathy?
* How does one go about setting up and maintaining schemes based around community helpers; what are the pitfalls and best practices and how do they differ from existing services?

Until we can come up with answers to these questions, either in general, or more particularly for the people in the communities within which we live and work, then care by the community can never become the norm.

I would hate, however, to give the impression that community care has been a flop. Quite the opposite. Examples of good community care can be increasingly found in many places, even if they have taken longer and involved much more effort to get under way than was originally hoped. Many are staffed by professional workers but ordinary men and women are also involved. These schemes offer a quality of life to handicapped people and their families which their predecessors of even a decade ago would not have dared to wish. The challenge now is to provide a better life for all.

WHO'S THERE TO CARE?

We should be clear on one thing at the outset. The community as a corporate body does not, nor *can* it, care for any of its members. Rather, the responsibility for care has to be assigned to individual members within the community. Often this happens by default.

Family care—In all the talk about new styles of services, let's not forget that many ordinary men and women are intimately involved in caring for the majority of mentally handicapped people in Britain and Ireland and it costs the State only a fraction of what it expends on specialist staff. This is the care provided by families of handicapped people.

Rather belatedly, our service systems have come to recognise:

* the importance of educating parents about, and involving them in programmes to foster the child's development;
* the parents' right to have an active role in decisions about their child's future;
* and, more radically, for parents to be consulted about and to influence the provision of services in general.

We still have some way to go before family involvement becomes widely practised.[14, 15] The merger of parental and professional interests is not easily achieved, even when they do start talking to one another.

But leaving all the responsibility for care with families is not the model of community care which I and others have in mind. Quite simply, the vast majority of parents do not have the resources to meet all the needs of their handicapped son or daughter. Of course, that goes for families with non-handicapped children as well. To sustain family care at optimum levels, support services for parents are required.

Specialist staffing—Over the years, but especially since the establishment of the Welfare State, the 'community' has enlisted—and paid—an increasing number of special people to do the job of looking after the handicapped: nurses, doctors, teachers, etc. Latterly the professional ranks have been swollen through an influx of new 'specialisms'. No one can dispute the tremendous contribution all have made and continue to make in producing a better life for mentally handicapped people. But reliance solely on 'specialist' care-givers is proving unsatisfactory for two main reasons:

1 *Costs.* Expansion of services to meet new needs—either in terms of new people requiring a service or of each person receiving all the services they need—is constrained because finance is not available to pay the necessary staff. The fact has to be faced that no society will ever have sufficient money to ensure that *all* mentally handicapped people receive *all* the services they need.[16]

In addition to arguing for a bigger share of the national cake, we must simultaneously explore ways of maximising the client-to-cost ratio so that more people can benefit from the same amount of money. Edgar Watson Howe put it more forthrightly when he wrote: 'People are always neglecting something they can do in trying to do something they can't do.'

2 *Quality and range of services.* There is an inevitable rigidity about any system which does not wish to exploit its workforce unfairly, yet at the same time has to ensure that they do the job for which they are paid. Hence it has proved more convenient to locate services centrally and to open them at stated times—convenient, that is, for service managers. If it does not suit mentally handicapped people or their families, then so be it.

Equally, it is not thought cost-effective to provide services for individuals or small groups of clients even on a short-term basis or to contemplate services occurring outside normal 'working hours', which would add an undue cost in overtime payments. The consequence is that the quality and range of services on offer is often pared down to the lowest common denominator.

The Independent Development Council[17] for people with mental handicap, summed it up this way: 'Excessive reliance on separate, specialist services is both expensive and wasteful and serves to segregate people with mental handicap from community life.'

A NEW STYLE OF SERVICE

There is a sense in which the professionalisation of services has become a victim of its own success. There is now a great deal of agreement on the style of service which people with mental handicaps most benefit from if they are to live their lives to the full, and it is far more than tender loving care.[18]

* *Individualised*—services should be organised to meet the needs of the individual rather than to cater for a group of people. A great deal of emphasis is now placed on having Individual Programme Plans for each client within the service.
* *Personalised*—services are provided to accord with the individual's needs, including social, emotional and recreational needs, and although a range of services may be on offer, not all will be needed by each client. Moreover, the essential feature of a service is not the building in which it is located but rather the people who are there to help.
* *Localised*—the service is available in the clients' neighbourhood so that there is a far greater chance of them remaining part of their community.
* *Normalised*—in the sense that disabled people are provided with a range of experiences which are commensurate with those of their able-bodied peers and, wherever possible, they should use existing general services, with extra help as they need it.

This style of service is far removed from that on which services have been [traditionally] based—special schools, adult training centres, hostels and hospitals, to name most of them. Many of the uncertainties and confusions in recent years probably stem from trying to reconcile an unchanged model of service with this new concept of clients' needs.

One promising solution is for specialist staff to forge partnerships with other groups in the community, who might help people with mental handicaps directly or assist their families on a person-to-person basis.

I do not pretend to have a blue-print for new service structures but I can be sure of one thing: it will have more in common with workers' co-operatives than with multi-national corporations or governmental bureaucracies. Sad to say, there are more bureaucrats organising services for disabled people than ever before and some of them more than live up to Brooks Atkinson's definition of the perfect bureaucrat, 'the man who manages to make no decisions and escape all responsibility.'

WHO ELSE COULD CARE?

If we take away the blinkers of precedent and ask who else in the community is available to care, the answer is not as depressing as it might first appear. I can think of three other groups in addition to specialist staff.

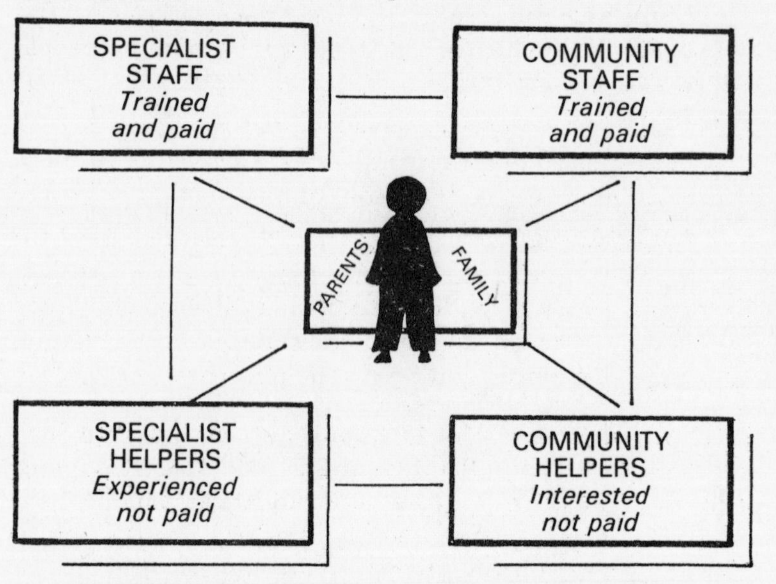

Staff available to help people who are mentally handicapped

Community staff—Here I have in mind staff employed in services for the community as a whole. This includes teachers in ordinary schools or colleges of further education, health visitors and local doctors, as well as other community workers, such as those involved in Youth Clubs, for example. They could share some of the helping, especially when the handicapping conditions are not too severe, the attraction being that often they will only be called upon to deal with one or two handicapped people at a time; they are available locally and they will facilitate the integration of the disabled person with his or her peers.

Such schemes are well established in many places although there is as yet no widespread consensus about the extent to which community staff can, should or must be used.

Specialist helpers—In the main these will be parents with experience of raising a mentally handicapped child, although the group could also include the former staff of disability services. Families often refer to the support they get from meeting other parents. Hence, at one level, this could take the form of self-help groups; with each participant providing some assistance to the others, even if it is only moral rather than practical support. Other schemes deploy parents in more direct helping relationships; providing short-term breaks for each other or acting as advisers on coming to terms with the child's disability and as instructors on home teaching methods. The value of such schemes is well documented, even though they have not yet been widely established.[19]

Community helpers—By far the largest group of potential helpers will be made up of ordinary women and men who are sufficiently interested and concerned to help the people whom they might describe as being 'less fortunate than themselves'. Of course voluntary effort has played, and continues to play, an important part in all personal and social services. Mainly, however, the role of the volunteer has been that of a fund-raiser, or else he—but more usually she—is seen as an adjunct or an assistant to the professional.

The new concept of 'community helper' is a far cry from the stereotype many people have of the volunteer.[2] First, helpers are recruited from a cross-section of ages and social backgrounds, men as well as women. Second, the aim is to deploy them in directly helping handicapped people or their families, often in community settings rather than in specialist centres such as schools or hostels. Third, the helpers might be contracted to undertake a particular task for a set period of time and, in recognition of this, they could receive some payment.

Fostering a child or adolescent is probably the best developed example of community helpers in action.[20, 21] In recent years a growing number of families have been willing to give a home to a mentally handicapped child when their natural parents were no longer able or willing to cope. Such schemes require diligent planning and monitoring by specialist staff, but the actual care is provided by people who have no training other than that obtained through rearing their own families, and no qualifications bar those of loving and caring for people.

Fostering, on the whole, has been a huge success: not only in the quality of care which the families provide for the child, but also in the value for money which they offer. It can be four times more costly for a child to live in a special centre than with a foster family.

PERSON-TO-PERSON SERVICES

Once we widen the concept of care-givers beyond family and specialist staff, then person-to-person services could become a reality for many more mentally handicapped people. They embody all the requirements outlined earlier for meeting the needs of disabled people and their families—they can be individualised, localised and personalised. Here are some examples of schemes known to me; all of which are 'staffed' by community or specialist helpers, supported by parents or specialist staff.

* *Home teaching*—volunteer 'teachers' visit a mentally

handicapped teenager or young adult at home to give individual tuition with skills such as reading or writing.

* *Home helps*—Community helpers, such as young people on work preparation courses, are allocated to a family for three days a week. They attend when the handicapped person returns from the day centre or school and stay until bedtime. They have particular responsibility to help with the care of the disabled member of the family, but inevitably they share the other chores of family life. Services like these enable families to cope and reduce the likelihood of admissions to full-time care.
* *Home breaks*—An alternative to taking handicapped adults or children into care for short stays, so that the family might have a break, is to place the person with another family. We have found that this works well with people who have had no previous experience of mental handicap, but it is especially successful when the host family is what I termed a 'specialist helper, e.g. a former member of staff or a person with a handicapped relative.[22]
* *Open employment*—The Pathway scheme,[23] developed by Mencap, facilitates the placement of mentally handicapped people in open employment by recruiting a 'helper' from the workforce who undertakes to keep an eye on the new employee and to smooth his or her integration with other workers. Under these arrangements there has been a dramatic increase in the number of sustained placements in open employment.
* *Evening classes*—Another demonstration project sponsored by Mencap[24] entailed recruiting people to accompany mentally handicapped adults to evening classes which were of mutual interest to both. Such schemes help to widen the social and recreational pursuits of disabled adults, many of whom lead very impoverished lives.

* *Independent living*—University students living away from home share accommodation with handicapped adults, who are fairly competent at looking after themselves but benefit from having somebody around in case they get into difficulties.[25] This arrangement eliminates the costs of employing care staff.

All these schemes were launched with the same basic presumption:

> *There are people in the community who are willing to be involved in helping mentally handicapped people, for little or no monetary reward*

The cynics and sceptics may well dismiss such people as fanatics, but so far they have been found in sufficient quantities and discovered to be so totally rational in thought and action as to make this presumption wholly reasonable. In fact, given the increased leisure time which people now have in western societies, some of it enforced through unemployment, there may never have been a better time to offer people opportunities for worthwhile, rewarding pursuits on a part-time or occasional basis.

THE IMPONDERABLES

Nonetheless, there are many imponderables to be cleared up before services utilising community helpers can become standard practice in the same way as specialist, segregated services are now established. This of course includes questions of funding and the redefining of staff roles, but we must also learn more about the community in which mentally handicapped people live and work.

Over the past five years, I and my colleagues, notably Bob McCormack and Jodie Walsh, have been engaged in a programme of service-related research studies which were first carried out in the city of Dublin but later extended to other places around Ireland by our counterparts in other services. As I mentioned in the Preface, the findings of our research programme are presented in three volumes, of which this is the first. Here the focus is on the results obtained from a fact-finding study into community perspectives on mental handicap. Details of community education strategies are given in the book *Breaking Barriers*,[1] while information about the setting up of schemes is contained in Jodie Walsh's book, *Let's Make Friends*.[2]

Two suburban housing estates were selected for the fact-finding study into community attitudes. In one estate, a day centre for mentally handicapped people was located; the other had a group home. The presence of a mental handicap service was crucial. Cnaan,[26] among others, has argued that communities 'under threat' give a more accurate appraisal of likely attitudes than those where mental handicap may be a distant phenomenon.

More than 600 individual interviews were completed with representative samples of residents, making it one of the most extensive and in-depth investigations undertaken in the field of community attitudes to mental handicap. This book details the results obtained.

Our aim is to equip you, the reader, with information of two sorts:

First, facts and figures about Irish people's experiences of, and their reactions to, mental handicap. Although we cannot guarantee that similar results will be obtained in your area, you will have some indication of how people might react.

In this book you will read about:

* The large proportion of mentally handicapped adults who are home- and family-bound when it comes to leisure activities (Chapter 2).
* The people in the community who are most likely to be in contact with disabled people in general and mentally handicapped people in particular (Chapter 4).
* What contacts took place between local people and

mentally handicapped adults attending a day centre in the community, or those living in a group home on a suburban housing estate (Chapter 4).

* People's perceptions of what it means to be mentally handicapped (Chapter 5).
* The sort of contacts which people are prepared to accept with mentally handicapped peers and which ones they consider are the most likely to occur (Chapter 6).
* The problems they could foresee arising if two adults with mental handicap lived next door to them (Chapter 7).
* The people in the community who are most interested in finding out more about mental handicap and their preferred ways of getting this information (Chapter 8).
* The type of work they would be interested in doing and the conditions they would like to see fulfilled (Chapter 9).

Secondly, we intend the books to be 'do-it-yourself' manuals. We want to equip you to carry out your own research and development work because each community is a unique amalgam of individuals, and what works in one place may flop in another. Hence, we give you details of how we set about surveying community attitudes, devising educational programmes and setting up new schemes so that you have guidelines for the actions you might undertake in your area to make community helper schemes become a reality.

In this book, we describe:

* The steps involved in carrying out a survey of community attitudes.
* Some of the pitfalls which have to be avoided in devising questions.
* How the data can be handled and analysed.
* 'Model' questionnaires which you might use as they stand or adapt as necessary.

THE OUTCOME

I realise that not all of you will be willing or able to embark upon such pursuits. To those who prefer to think of it as someone else's responsibility, with yours the task to 'pressurise' them to do it, I wish you good luck.

Others will be so engrossed in keeping services going that they feel they have no time left to explore other ways of working. I believe that is neither in their own best interests nor in those of their clients because, as the Chinese say, 'it is better to light a candle, than to curse the darkness'.

This book is for the rest of you, and I hope that's most of you, who want to see more links between mentally handicapped people and their neighbours in the community, and who are willing to take steps to bring this about. No longer can you be accused of being day-dreamers, idealists or irrational fanatics. Reality has been tested, planning can begin. In Eric Hoffer's words, we can now offer an 'around-the-corner type of hope' to families and mentally handicapped people 'that prompts people to action', instead of 'the distant hope which acts as an opiate'.

2 Who's Mentally Handicapped?

When I go to the shops for the paper, small children—they kind of look at me.

Man, in his 30s, who has Down's Syndrome

People with mental handicap may look different and some may act oddly. But could it be that people's images have been distorted by their lack of familiarity and unwarranted fears?

I recall a story from my primary school days, with the moral that mirrors never lie. Set in mediaeval days when mirrors were a luxury item, it concerned a narcissistic young king who had grown fat through overindulgence and lazy living. On looking at himself in a mirror one day, he was appalled and distressed. However, a wise counsellor at the court assured him that the palace mirror was faulty. The only true mirror in the kingdom had been stolen some years before and was rumoured to have been abandoned in the hills. The king was determined to find it and for days, nay months, thereafter he travelled far and wide searching for the mirror and, as the weeks passed, he became ever fitter and healthier. At last success was his, and when he looked in the mirror, sure enough he saw the handsome reflection which he knew to be true.

It was of course, no coincidence that the wise counsellor happened to be with the king on the day the discovery was made. He had smuggled the palace mirror under his cloak and left it conveniently ready for the king to discover. The clever ploy had worked and, like all good stories, this one ended with the king realising that it was he who had changed—the reflection was always true.

The community's image of people with disabilities has to

be set against reality. If we were to hold up a mirror to adults with mental handicap, living in the community, what reflection would we get? Surprisingly little accurate information is available. Past studies were more concerned with institutional populations[27] and recent ones have focused only on subgroups, such as people attending Adult Training Centres.[28]

This chapter describes a population of mentally handicapped adults, living in the community in two districts of Dublin city. You can read about:

* their ages, additional handicaps and, most importantly, what they can and cannot do for themselves;
* their family backgrounds; the services they attend and their leisure persuits;
* their care-givers' perceptions of the services they will need in the future.

It is likely that a somewhat similar picture would emerge for other cities and counties. This happened when the survey was repeated in County Kildare.[29] As in the story of the king, this 'true' image may not be seen by people from the community, unless they get more 'exercise', principally through contact with people who are mentally handicapped.

MENTALLY HANDICAPPED ADULTS LIVING IN THE COMMUNITY

The Medico-Social Research Board of Ireland was commissioned by the Eastern Health Board to carry out a survey of adult mentally handicapped persons living in Dublin city and its environs, as a basis for planning future services.[30] St Michael's House Research Department was invited to assist.

We opted for a population study, that is, we would attempt to locate ALL the mentally handicapped people living within a designated area. Two of the city's eight community care areas were chosen for the survey.

Every attempt was made to identify all persons over 15 years of age who were suspected of being mentally handicapped. The state disability records were checked and everyone registered in these areas as being 'mentally handicapped'—either solely or in combination with another condition, such as physical handicap or psychiatric illness—was contacted. This yielded 90 per cent of the survey population. Specialist services both within and outside the designated community care areas were also contacted and this yielded an additional seven per cent. Finally, checks through psychiatric registers and local contacts yielded the remaining three per cent of the survey population.

In all, 712 persons were identified: 292 in one area and 420 in the other. All the people in the first area were contacted, along with a one-in-two random sample in the second. Interviewing showed that 150 people out of 712 originally listed were not mentally handicapped. Thus, the final population consisted of 562 persons; an administrative incidence of about one in every 250 Dublin citizens. Or put another way, in a neighbourhood (electoral ward) of 3,000 people, one could expect to find around 12 adults who were mentally handicapped.

Interviews—All the information was obtained through individual structured interviews in the homes of the mentally handicapped people. Repeated calls were made if necessary. Most interviews were with a parent (73 per cent) or a family member (20 per cent) but in seven per cent of instances, the handicapped person was the respondent. Interviews lasted, on average, around 45 minutes.

Characteristics of the adults—There were more males (57 per cent) than females (43 per cent); the reverse of the ordinary population, where, according to the last census, there are 53 per cent females.

The oldest person in the survey was 64 years of age, the youngest 15 years. On the whole, there were many more younger people.

Over half were between 15 and 25 years of age

A further 20 per cent were between 25 and 34 years and the remaining 30 per cent were 35 to 64 years of age. Two main factors could account for this. Community care services only started during the past 20 years, thus more of the older age groups are in residential settings; and latterly there is an increased life-expectancy for mentally handicapped people due to better medical care.

Additional handicaps—About one quarter of the adults surveyed were reported to have an additional handicap, such as recurring epileptic fits (nine per cent); inability to talk (seven per cent); inability to walk unaided (six per cent); little or no use of hands (five per cent); marked hearing loss with aid prescribed (three per cent); or difficulty in seeing, which gave rise to problems in mobility (two per cent).

In all, one in six people were reported to have one of these handicaps; four and a half per cent reported two and three per cent had three or more. But:

Three-quarters had no additional handicaps

For the majority of people (70 per cent) no diagnosis was given but 12 per cent had Down's Syndrome and 18 per cent were said to have cerebral palsy or hydrocephalus.

ABILITIES

A specially developed index[31] was used in the survey to ascertain the ability levels of the mentally handicapped adults, particularly in the self-care and social skills areas. This would enable us to find out how capable they were of looking after themselves, and how many needed someone's help.

The index covered many of the domains tapped by more extensive indices of social functioning, such as the *Adaptive Behaviour Scale*,[32] but used a simpler four or five rating scale within 12 ability areas. (A copy is given in the Appendix.)

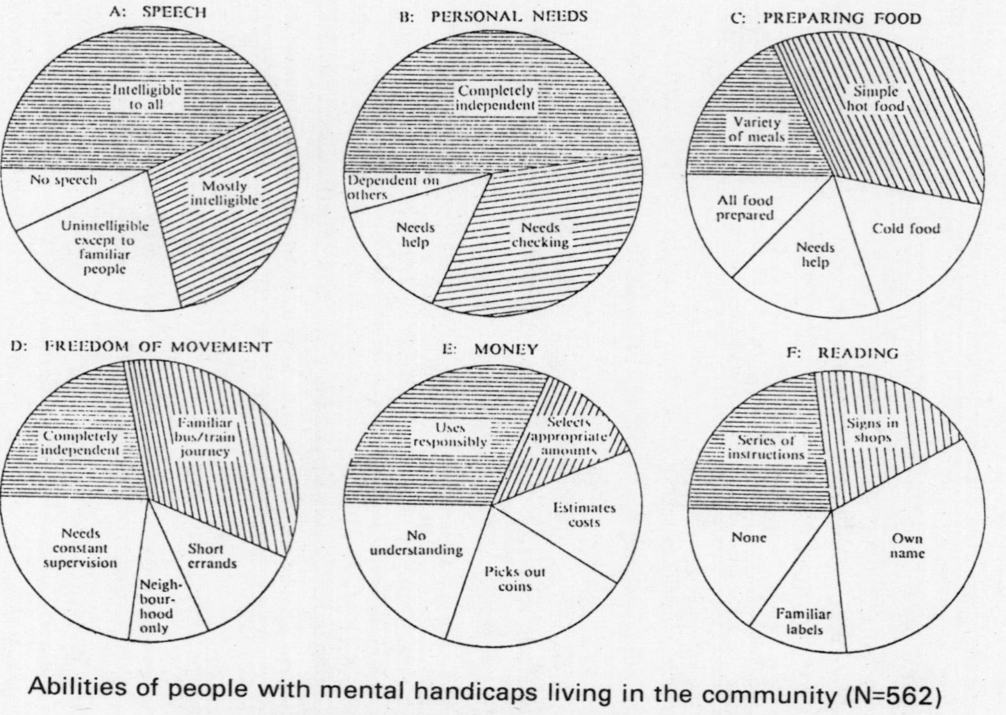

Abilities of people with mental handicaps living in the community (N=562)

Reprinted from *Mental Handicap* by kind permission

Here is a summary of people's abilities within six skill areas: communication, personal needs, preparing food, freedom of movement, money and reading.

Speech—Over 70 per cent of adults had intelligible speech, although some had difficulty in fluency. Nearly 60 per cent were capable of remembering and carrying out instructions which could be done straight away. Only ten per cent gave no response when talked to, other than their own name.

Self-care—As the Figure shows, nearly half of the adults were able to take care of all their personal needs completely independently; only one in five were dependent on others for help—for example 14 per cent needed help with feeding and drinking. In addition, over half could prepare some meals for themselves, and two in five were capable of doing most jobs around the home without supervision—making beds, doing dishes, cleaning floors. There was, however, a significantly different pattern for males and females: 64 per cent of females could manage the household tasks, but only 50 per cent of males. Conversely, 21 per cent of males but only ten per cent of females were judged incapable of doing household jobs.

Freedom of movement—Sex differences were also apparent in the extent to which adults could find their way around their neighbourhood. The Figure gives the overall percentages obtained, but in fact 64 per cent of males and only 47 per cent of females were travelling independently or using public amenities alone. Conversely, 27 per cent of the females were rated as needing constant supervision, compared to 20 per cent of the males.

Interestingly, there were comparable sex differences on the mobility scale. Here, 73 per cent of males but only 57 per cent of females were rated as being capable of running and climbing with no difficulty, whereas 37 per cent of females and only 21 per cent of males tired easily or found stairs difficult. The percentage of those requiring help to walk were comparable for both sexes.

Community skills—As the Figure illustrates, nearly half the adults were capable of coping with everyday money transactions and reading common signs. Nearly 60 per cent could tell the time in hours and minutes. Just over 50 per cent could write their own name and address without help.

Age effects—The same pattern of abilities generally held for all the age groups, but there were two exceptions. Firstly, more older people were rated capable of doing household tasks—47 per cent of the over 25s compared with 26 per cent of the under 25s. It would appear that in this area, abilities and/or expectations increase with age.

Secondly, fewer of the over 40s were capable of walking, running and climbing stairs—53 per cent compared with 70 per cent of the under 40s.

Four sub-groupings

As you have seen, there is a wide range of abilities among a population labelled 'mentally handicapped'. No report can do justice to their individuality, but as a step towards it we found it helpful to subdivide the people into four groups, based on a factor analysis of the abilities index.

High ability

Nearly one third of the adults were able to look after all their self-care needs, both personal and around the house, were able communicators and had mastered sufficient skills in literacy and numeracy to deal with daily living.

Low ability

By contrast, just under one in five were 'severely' handicapped people, needing assistance with self-care, having difficulties in communicating with others and having no literacy or numeracy skills.

Over 50 per cent fell between these two extremes

Competent in self-care

One in five were capable of looking after their self-care needs but experienced difficulty in communication and/or literacy and numeracy.

Assistance with self-care

Nearly one in three adults required assistance with self-care needs, mainly because of additional physical handicaps, but they were competent in communication and/or literacy and numeracy.

This classification, I stress again, does not mean that all the people within a sub-group are the same; far from it. But these results suggest that:

PEOPLE WITH MENTAL HANDICAP ARE GENERALLY MUCH MORE COMPETENT THAN THE COMMUNITY PERCEIVES THEM TO BE[33]

Family background

Nine out of ten of the adults were living with their families

To be precise, 56 per cent were at home with both parents, 21 per cent with their mother only, three per cent with their father only and a further 11 per cent were being cared for by a family member. Only six per cent were living in a hostel run by a voluntary organisation and three per cent were living alone.

In terms of the occupation of the 'care person', 14 per cent could be classed within the professional/supervisory categories, 29 per cent as skilled-manual, 19 per cent as semi-skilled, and 37 per cent as unskilled/routine. Two thirds of the care-givers were under 60 years of age; one in five were between 60 and 69 years but as many as 12 per cent were over 70 years.

SERVICES ATTENDED

One in 20 of the adults were working in open employment and eight in 20 were attending day services, the most common being a long-term sheltered workshop (21 per cent), a short-term training centre (seven per cent) and a day special care unit for severely handicapped adults (six per cent).

But those quick at doing sums will have realised that, as Bayley[5] found in Sheffield:

> *More than half were at home most of the day*

Various reasons were given for not accepting a day placement offered by the mental handicap services—the mentally handicapped person was thought to be too old; he or she preferred to remain at home; the service was not financially advantageous; the level of work was not appropriate. Only four per cent of respondents were unaware that day service facilities were available.

LEISURE PURSUITS

Most mentally handicapped adults spent their leisure time with their parents (64 per cent) or their brothers or sisters (57 per cent).

> *Nearly half spent ALL their leisure time activities with the family*

Just over 30 per cent went to community activities such as cinemas and swimming baths. Nearly 40 per cent were said to share their leisure time with a friend. But only 20 per cent, mainly those in the *high ability* group, had a non-handicapped friend.

FUTURE NEEDS

Finally, the families were asked to give their opinions about their anticipated need for services in the future.

Day Service[30]—45 per cent of families felt that their mentally handicapped member needed some form of day service that was different from the present situation. The most frequently mentioned were: open employment or short-term training (59 per cent); long-term sheltered workshops (28 per cent); and further education (two per cent). Not surprisingly, it was the people from the *high ability* group who mainly required open employment or short-term training.

Residential Care[34]—Five per cent of families said they were in immediate need of this service due to a family 'crisis' and one quarter felt that they would require long-term residential care some time in the future. Over one quarter felt that they would make use of short-term/crisis care placements if they were available.

The need for some form of residential care facility was strongest with the *low ability* group, nearly half of the families mentioning it compared with only one in seven of families in the *high ability* group.

In general the majority of families envisaged the mentally handicapped person remaining in the community, and being cared for by a member of the family (37 per cent) or looking after himself (17 per cent).

Recreation[35]—The families' perceptions of improvements in the recreational area were more circumscribed, e.g. 47 per cent made no suggestions, ten per cent stated that there should be improvements, but gave no specific instances. The suggestion made most frequently was for more clubs, and these would not just be for handicapped people (21 per cent). Other suggestions were for more sporting activities (17 per cent), night-classes (eight per cent), clubs specifically for handicapped people (nine per cent) and more local community facilities (two per cent).

Could a caring community meet some or all of these needs?

CONCLUSIONS

The picture which emerges from this survey belies the popular image of mentally handicapped adults which in the past has often been determined by images of people in residential settings.

* The majority are capable of looking after all their personal needs and only a minority—less than 20 per cent—are dependent on others for help.
* Most can communicate adequately through speech with just over one in four having difficulty.
* Over half are capable of getting around on public transport and all but a small percentage are imobile.
* As many as one in three are capable of simple reading and can handle money responsibly.
* In three out of four instances, care-givers envisaged the mentally handicapped person continuing to live in the local community.

However, this hopeful scenario contrasts markedly with the picture which emerged of their lifestyle:

* Over half were not at work, nor were they attending any form of day service.
* Only a minority spent their leisure time with friends or in community facilities. To a large extent they were 'home and family' bound.
* Fewer than one in five were reported to have a non-handicapped friend, and these invariably came from the higher ability groupings.

Here's how some of these people attending a special workshop for mentally handicapped people described their lifestyle:

I had friends when I was small, friends down the road. They are grown up now, they are working.

I used to want to be a guard or a barber . . . but I just grew up and forgot about it.

I don't go out—just watch telly . . . I like to look after my mother and make tea for her and myself, and light the fire for her.

I have loads of friends. I wish I could get to know a lot more people.

A fundamental issue is whether these people are offered help through services specifically for mentally handicapped people, or whether these are better provided through services aimed at the community in general.

Once the latter course of action is adopted, even if on a small scale, we must try to learn more about the community and the public's perceptions of mentally handicapped people. Michael Bayley[5] reasoned thus:

> Care out of the community need not concern itself with the community from which it is removing the client. Even care in the community need not concern itself overmuch with what the community is or the way it functions. But care by the community demands understanding of what it is, sympathy with the way it works and insight into the way the community can help.

The spotlight must shift to the community.

3 Who's Who in the Community?

> I'd go for a long walk if I was let . . . but there is too much traffic on the roads . . . I'd prefer out in the country.
>
> *Woman living at home*

As with many other cities in Britain and Europe, Dublin's fair city is not a uniform entity but rather an amalgam of many different communities. Some have their roots in villages which once circled the city but are now absorbed by it, whereas others are newly planned suburbs carved out of farmland. No one locality could claim to be representative of the city as a whole and we would be foolish to pretend so. One of the strengths of the community care philosophy is the richness and uniqueness which each community can contribute to the well-being of its members; a contrast to the blandness often found in uniformity.

In this chapter we describe:

* the two communities which took part in the study so that you can get a fuller picture of their background. You should then be able to judge how alike they are to the communities you live and work among;
* the steps involved in carrying out a study of this sort. Unlike journal reports we spare you none of the colourful details!
* the four previous studies carried out in Britain and Ireland which are used throughout the book as a check on whether the Dublin findings apply to other areas.

A TALE OF TWO SUBURBS

Our story begins with one community located in the

northern suburbs of Dublin city. Following World War Two—a period known in Ireland as the 'Emergency'—there was a rapid expansion of public housing estates. Many were occupied by newly-married couples who found work in the recently developed light industries.

Most have now reared their families, but they continue to live on the same estate. Some are now owner-occupiers because the Corporation gave them the option to buy their houses, but most still pay rent.

It was in one of these communities that St Michael's House decided to open a Day Centre for some 60 adults who were judged to be so severely handicapped that they were unable to attend long-term training centres, where contract work for local industries was undertaken. This Centre served the whole of the north side of the city and clients were transported from home in special minibuses, some from as far as five miles away.

As the map of the area shows, the Centre is located at the heart of the small housing estate, in prefabricated buildings which had formerly housed the local primary school. The school had recently moved to adjacent, purpose-built premises.

Two years after the Day Centre had opened we embarked upon the community study. The area was ideal for our purposes:

* The district formed a compact, well-defined community that had been long-established.
* In the middle of the community—almost literally—was a service for adult mentally handicapped people. Hence the people in this neighbourhood would have had more opportunity than most Dubliners to come into contact with mental handicap. It has been argued[36, 37] that their perceptions and attitudes would be more realistic in that they are based not on supposition, but rather on the experience of living with the 'problem'—in some small sense at least.
* We had access to the names of all the people over 18 years of age living in that locality. In case you think we had something special going for us, all it meant was a trip to the Post Office to consult the electoral register. Fortuitously, this estate formed an electoral ward which meant that we could easily take a random sample of names from the register.

And so we were ready to begin. Details of what we did, and why, will come later in the chapter, but I want to jump ahead to when we started to get some of the results. As you will read in Chapter 4, we were surprised at how few people in the area were aware of the Centre. We were intrigued to know if this would happen in another area, so we decided to repeat the survey in a second community.

Our choice of a second area was constrained mainly because in Dublin we could find only a few Centres for mentally handicapped adults which were located in housing areas. We finally opted for a relatively new private housing estate in which there was a Group Home for seven adults who were moderately or mildly mentally handicapped.

The home consisted of two adjacent semi-detached houses, joined internally, and it was opened soon after the estate was built, some 12 years ago. Unlike the district where the Day Centre was located, the house was on the periphery of the estate although adjacent to a well-used footpath leading to the shops and bus stops.

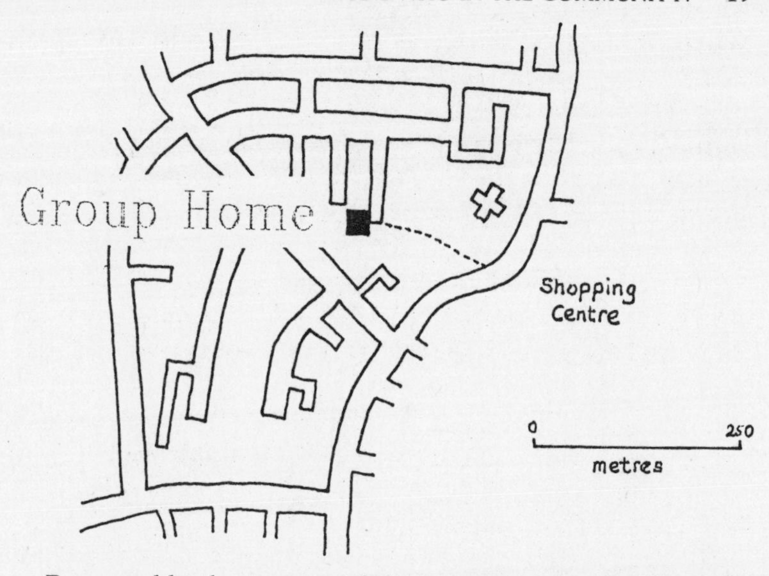

But would it be meaningful to compare the results from the two communities? Past research[1, 38] had suggested that age and sex had a crucial influence on people's attitudes. If our two areas were equated on these variables it would cut down the number of explanations for differences in the perceptions of the communities, assuming that they did differ. Hence in Area 2 we took a quota sample, stratified by age and sex according to the sample characteristics from Area 1. But as you will read later, there were still marked differences between the two communities. In fact, when you think of all the variables which go to make up a community, it would be surprising if there were no differences.

Finally, the data given in Chapter 9, on the voluntary work which people in the community might be willing to do, was collected through interviews carried out in the local shopping centres of each neighbourhood with quota samples stratified by sex and age of 100 people from each locality.

Samples

As I have said, the study began in the neighbourhood

where the Day Centre was located. A random sample of 321 people was taken from the electoral register and we managed to interview 279 of them—87 per cent. In the area of the Group Home, a quota sample of 150 people, matched in age and sex to the random sample, was used, giving a grand total of 419 individual interviews.

As the table below shows, the age structure in our sample differed from the Irish population as a whole (1985 Census)[39] chiefly in a preponderance of people under 29 and in their 40s. However, this is explicable given the history of the housing estate.

Percentages of people at different age levels

Ages	*Percentage in sample*	*Percentage Irish adult population*
18–19	17	6
20–29	35	23
30–39	12	19
40–49	25	14
50 plus	12	38

It is highly unlikely that any local community will reflect the national age structure. Yet, as you will read in later chapters, age does influence people's perceptions and attitudes to mental handicap. Hence it could be important for you to determine the age structure in the communities with which you deal.

We also had an excess of females in our areas—57 per cent to 43 per cent—whereas the national balance is 53 per cent to 47 per cent. About half the discrepancy was due to more males being uncontactable or unwilling to be interviewed, but the areas still had more females than males.

Community Life

Part of our interview was given over to collecting details about the person's involvement in community life (see questionnaire in Appendix). This enabled us to learn more

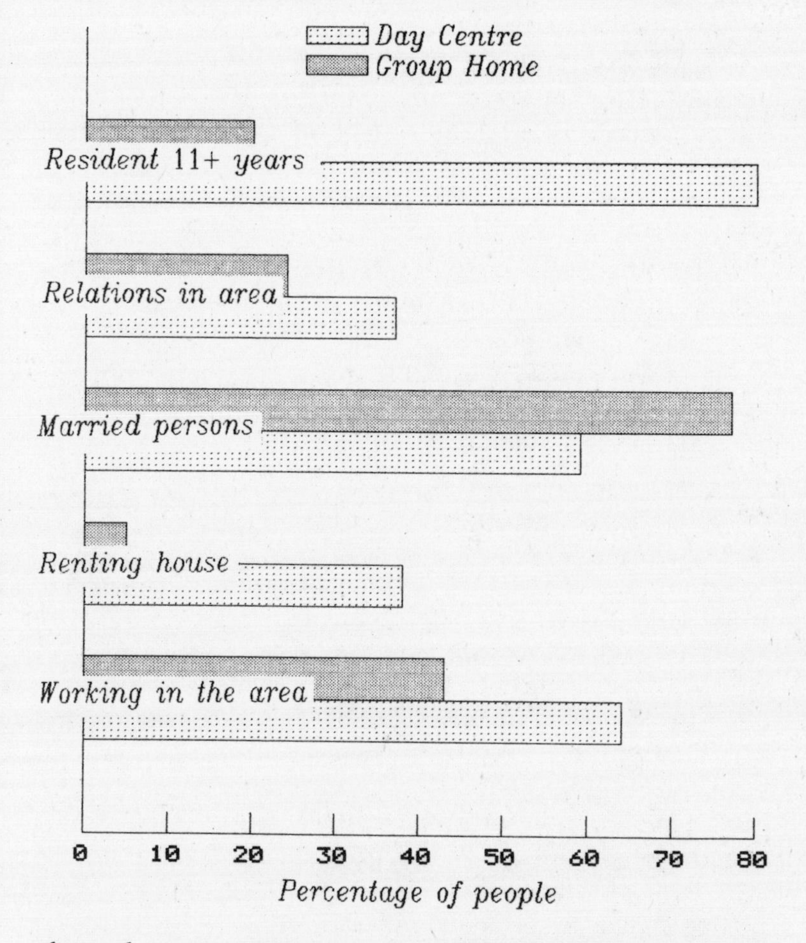

about the two communities and, although we had matched the samples on age and sex, we soon discovered that significant differences remained between them. Some of the more striking ones are outlined in the Figure.

We made use of a statistical procedure called Discriminant Analysis[40] which helps to detect the root differences between two groups. In the case of our two areas these were the length of time people had lived in the area and the number of families related to each other. These are root differences in the sense that they help to account for other differences, such as the total number of families people know in an area.

Overall, the area with the Day Centre was a longer established community than the one with the Group Home, which meant that people tended to know other families or had relations living in the neighbourhood. Moreover a higher number of people worked or studied in the area.

By contrast, the area with the Group Home had a higher proportion of married people and all but five per cent were buying their own homes.

There were no differences between the two areas in the age at which the residents left school (nearly two-thirds at 15 years or earlier and only one in 13 had gone to tertiary level), or in the proportion of families with children under 12 in the house (60 per cent).

Community involvement—Overall, the degree to which people were involved in activities within both areas was quite low—our definition was that they could walk to them within 15 minutes. The figures neatly divided into thirds—one third reported no involvement; one third went to one activity and the final third to two or more activities.

At the risk of perpetuating Irish stereotypes, by far the most popular community pursuit—engaged in by nearly half the neighbourhood—was going to the local pub. One in five people stated they went regularly.

Attendance at residents' association meetings and local clubs were the next most popular (15 per cent in total, but nearly all went regularly to the clubs whereas the majority attended the residents' association meetings only occasionally). Bingo (12 per cent), discos or dances (11 per cent), evening classes (seven per cent) and voluntary work (6 per cent) were also cited, and a few individuals (less than three per cent) attended prayer groups or political party meetings.

Obviously, level of participation in community pursuits

is determined to some extent by their availability within an area. Many of the people we interviewed bemoaned the lack of facilities—for example, neither area had a cinema, youth club or sports centre. Communities with better facilities for their residents might well show higher levels of involvement, although with so many people now owning cars, it is much easier for them to travel beyond their community for leisure as well as work.

Impressions of a Community

These facts and figures tell us something of the two communities, but I would be the first to admit that in themselves they say little about whether these people felt they belonged to a community or merely lived in a neighbourhood. There are other interesting questions about the communities which we would have loved to ask—but that would have left less time for the questions about mental handicap.

The data to hand is open to interpretation. The community optimist could find much to gladden the heart—for example, two-thirds participating in at least one activity within the area—whereas the cynic may feel the figures bear out Cabeu's dictum: 'the optimist proclaims that we live in the best of all possible worlds; the pessimist fears this is true.'

We certainly came away with a greater appreciation of the difficulties in describing how groups of people relate to each other. For example, we know nothing about the extent of their contacts with neighbours—do they go beyond the exchange of pleasantries?—or what they would be prepared to do in personally helping out a neighbour. For instance, would a person be prepared to cook a meal for an elderly neighbour or would they see that as the duty of his family . . . the church . . . the Social Services Department or what? And why it is that some people feel a sense of responsibility to their neighbours and others do not.

Answers to these and other questions would give us a better understanding as to how mentally handicapped people might best remain or become members of a community. There is certainly no shortage of further research projects. And we might even discover that it is not just mentally handicapped people who stand to benefit.

CARRYING OUT THE SURVEY

The popular image of researchers busily examining computer printouts and crying 'Eureka!' is a far cry from the reality of most projects, which invariably involve much routine, even mundane administrative tasks such as compiling lists of names, drawing up different versions of the questionnaire, conducting interviews *ad nauseam*—or so it seems at the time—transforming people's answers to numbers for computer analysis—over 40,000 in this study—and finally getting the computer to do what you want it to do. After all that, we have the chance to behave like Archimedes, although few of us have the energy or inclination to run out into the streets to proclaim our discoveries.

Here is a run down on the steps we had to go through in carrying out the study:

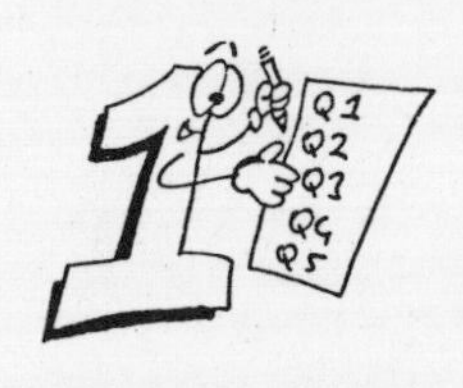

Assembling the questionnaire

From reading previous studies, we could formulate a list of possible questions we might use. To this were added 'new' questions which we felt were relevant.

We then tried out a preliminary version of the questionnaire with the unsuspecting people living in a housing estate adjacent to our Research Unit. This enabled us to discover which questions were working as we intended and which needed to be altered because of ambiguities or misunderstandings.

The layout of the final version of the questionnaire was then designed; it was typed, photocopied and collated. The pile of questionnaires used in the study stood 15 inches tall and weighed 10 kilos.

Selecting names to interview

The procedures were different in the two areas. In Area 1 we extracted a sample of 321 names from the electoral register by using random number tables. The total was arrived at through the use of a standard formula* that enables you to be 95 per cent confident that the sample will be representative of the whole population. If you want to be 99 per cent certain, a different figure goes into the equation and the result is a greater number of people in the sample.

The randomly selected names were listed by streets and given to the interviewers who asked for each person by name at the house. If the person was deceased or had moved out of the area he or she was replaced by a person from the 'reserve list' which had been drawn up.

If the person was not in when the interviewer called, up to three repeat calls were made before the person was declared uncontactable. These people were not replaced, nor were the small number (14 in all) who refused to be interviewed. Over all, we were able to contact 87 per cent of the sample—279 people.

In Area 2 the procedures were different because we opted for a quota sample. Here we calculated the number of people by sex and age groups whom we wanted to interview and then called on houses within the estate until we had filled up our quotas—150 people all told. As in Area 1, many more calls had to be made to houses to arrive at this total.

Recruiting interviewers

You do not have to be a wizard at mental arithmetic to realise that it would take one person a long time to complete more than 400 interviews plus an indeterminate number of extra calls. Our estimate was nearly half a year, working five evenings a week.

$$5\%^* = 1.96^* \left(\sqrt{\frac{2,500}{n}}\right) \times \left(1 - \frac{n}{N}\right)$$

n = sample size N = population size

(*For 1% level of confidence, replace with 1% and 2.57 respectively)

The alternative was much more attractive—the more interviewers the quicker it could be done. It also meant that there would be less chance of people in the areas talking to each other about the survey and perhaps biasing the answers of people interviewed later. Hence we coaxed, cajoled and begged colleagues to help, opting where possible for those with research experience. All were briefed on using the interview schedule, the use of probe questions and recording answers.

However, there was a limit to the amount of time which our volunteer helpers could give us, so in the end, the bulk of the interviews were done by research staff or students on placement in the Research Unit.

Interviews

Most of the interviewing was done at weekends or in the evening; the best times to catch people at home. In all, 429 individual interviews were completed, lasting on average about 15 minutes and usually carried out on door-steps or in hallways but occasionally by the fireside—bliss!

The interview commenced with the statement, 'I'm from the University'. The University reference was chosen so as not to bias respondents and it was genuine. Part of the study would be used for a Master's degree by one of the students attached to St Michael's Research Unit. All interviewers carried a signed letter of identification from the Research Director.

After the interview, respondents were given a printed sheet of paper thanking them for helping with the research and giving a telephone number they could contact if they wanted further information about the study. In the event, no one telephoned.

Data Coding

It is often forgotten that computers, for all their speed and accuracy, suffer under a great disability—they can only digest numbers. Hence all the replies people gave to our questions had to be transformed into rows of numbers and these in turn had to be entered into the computer through a keyboard. These operations are tedious in the extreme, but given the quantity of data we had, there was no other way of coping but feeding the computer.

The risk of mistakes occurring in this process is quite high—a 3 can easily be read for an 8 or a line of numbers gets omitted. Hence checks and double-checks have to be made of the coded data to try to ensure its accuracy.

Data Analysis

The other delaying fact about computers is that you have to tell them what to do with all the numbers. Fortunately the magic letters SPSS provide a ready solution. They stand for *Statistical Package for the Social Sciences*,[40] which consists of a whole range of ready-made programmes for analysing survey data. This package, or similar ones, are available at most university computer installations and a version for use on personal computers has recently been marketed.

Computer packages are a double-edged sword—the temptation is to run many more analyses than you really need to; the consequence being that the pile of computer print-out grows ever higher, your computer bill increases and you put off the day when you get down to writing up the results of what you have found.

Sharing the findings

Without this step, all of the foregoing would come to nought. The true value of research lies in sharing the findings with others who could benefit from them—hence this book. But other ways can be used as well—talks, lectures to students and articles.

I confess, however, to letting one group down: the people who took part in the study. At the end of the interview we asked, 'Are there any comments you would like to make about the topics we have touched on in this survey?' A number of people—typically males in their teens or 20s—commented: 'Interested to know the findings of the survey'; 'Will I get the results of the survey?'; 'I'd like to hear the outcome of it all'.

I cannot imagine them running out to buy this book. Maybe some of the media coverage at its launching will let them know that their contribution was both valuable and valued.

COMPARISONS WITH OTHER SURVEYS

Finally, a word for the sceptics who may be thinking that our survey is of little or no relevance to them because they are living and working in Durham, Dundee or Dublin, Canada and not in Dublin, Ireland. One way of allaying your fears is to compare our results with those obtained in previous studies.

There are four main studies to which I shall make reference in subsequent chapters. These are:

Irish National Opinion Poll[41]—During the International Year of Disabled People in 1981, the Market Research Bureau of Ireland, on behalf of the Health Education Bureau, conducted a national poll within the Irish Republic involving a quota sample of 758 adults aged 15 years and over.

Mencap Poll[42]—The Royal Society for Mentally Handicapped Children and Adults (Mencap) commissioned a study on British attitudes to the mentally handicapped in February, 1982, undertaken by Market and Opinion Research International (MORI). They used two quota samples of adults, aged 15 years and over, living throughout Great Britain and totalling 1,909 people.

London neighbourhood survey[43]—A one-in-four random sample of residents—totalling 244—were interviewed individually. All lived in the six streets adjacent to a community hostel run by a voluntary organisation for 14 people, nine of whom were mentally handicapped men and women. The people in the area had previously been surveyed in 1977, prior to the hostel opening, and again in 1980.

West of Ireland survey[44]—In 1985, a random sample of households were chosen from four rural towns in the west of Ireland in which a day training centre had opened recently along with group homes. In all, 135 people were interviewed, no more than one adult per house, with sex and age group randomly assigned prior to entry.

Although our literature search turned up other studies, these were either not directly relevant to the topic of mental handicap or their samples were not comparable. However these are referenced[45-49] so that you have the chance to read the reports and to make up your own mind.

Needless to add, we learned from all of them and we incorporated or adapted the 'best' questions as well as inventing a few of our own. Nonetheless, I think we can rightly claim that our survey is the most extensive yet undertaken. Still, you can be the judge of that. Here are the results.

4 Who Knows?

> I don't go out—just watch telly . . . I like to look after my mother and make tea for her and myself, and light the fire for her.
>
> *Woman attending a day centre in Dublin*

An Australian visitor to Ireland told me once that she had seen more mentally handicapped people on the streets of Dublin than in any other city she had visited on her world tour. I was not sure whether to be insulted or proud of my adopted city. It is true that in Ireland we do have a relatively greater proportion of people with mental handicap per head of the population, but then again, we have been less inclined to shut people away in large institutions. Both factors could explain why mentally handicapped people are more frequently spotted by visitors.

Having disabled people out-and-about in the community is no guarantee that they are better known or understood by local people. Yet this presumption is frequently made by advocates of community services. Equally, we should not assume that members of the public have met and talked with disabled people. Previous surveys suggest that only a minority have done so. Yet the attitudes of these people are possibly quite different from those of their fellow citizens who have no experience of disability.

Hence our investigation began by getting answers to the following questions:

* Who, in the community, are the people most likely to be in contact with disabled people in general, and mentally handicapped people in particular?

* What sort of contacts have they had with disabled people, and where have they taken place?
* Do people in the housing estates know about the Day Centre or Group Home in their area?
* What contacts are there between local people and the mentally handicapped adults attending the Day Centre and the Group Home?

The answers, particularly to the latter two questions, will probably surprise you.

WHO KNOWS DISABLED PEOPLE?

HALF THE POPULATION HAVE NEVER MET A DISABLED PERSON

THREE-QUARTERS HAVE NEVER MET A MENTALLY HANDICAPPED PERSON

Hard to believe these findings isn't it? When disability is your life's work—whether as a parent or professional—you cannot imagine that it makes so little impact on other people's lives. What is routine and familiar to you is strange and unusual to them. We live in worlds apart from our neighbours.

We asked our people two questions. The first enquired about their contacts with 'disabled children and adults' and then, later in the questionnaire, we asked, 'What contact have you had with mentally handicapped adults?' For both questions we gave the same choice of answers and people selected the alternative which they felt best described their contacts. For instance:

No contact at all
Just seen them around
Occasional meetings or chats
Close, regular contact.

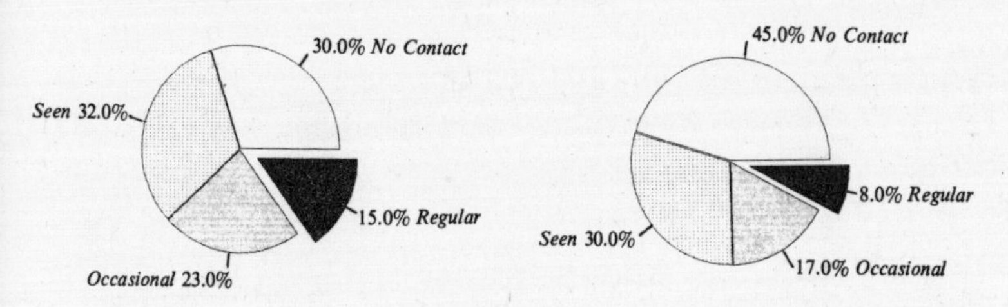

As you can see, the pattern of results was similar for both handicap groups but people are more likely to have had contact with disabled people in general than with mentally handicapped adults. This is not too surprising. For a start there are more disabled people around and they are more likely to remain in the community rather than living in residential care. A proportion will have become disabled through accident, infirmity or ageing, and their neighbourhood contacts may have been maintained.

By contrast, mentally handicapped people are fewer in number. Many have left their neighbourhoods to live in special centres and few will have attended local schools or played outside in the streets. People do not have the same opportunities to get to know them. Thus only one in 12 report being in regular contact with a mentally handicapped person compared with about one in seven regularly in contact with a disabled person.

We were also able to explore the extent of overlap in people's contacts with disabled and mentally handicapped people. This is the picture which emerged:

24 per cent no contact with either mentally or physically disabled people

32 per cent have seen one or other or both around

27 per cent report occasional contact with one or other or both

17 per cent have regular contact with one or other or both.

Confirmation, then, that only half the population are likely to have had contact with a handicapped person and at best only one in six are regularly in touch with a disabled person. *Few* know—is the answer to who knows?

Who's most likely to have had contact?—Only one clear characteristic emerged. The people most likely to have had contact with disabled people are those who report knowing a lot of families in their neighbourhood (i.e. 16 or more). More than a third of this group have been in contact with mentally handicapped adults, whereas it is less than one in five for the people knowing few families.

Women were no more likely than were men to have had contact, nor did people's age make any significant difference, although there was a tendency for 40–49-year-olds to have had more contact with mentally handicapped people.

As we shall see later, this picture changes when it comes to contacts with the local centre (see p. 76).

National polls—But, I hear you say, could it be that the people in these housing estates are unusual . . . are they a typical sample?

The results of opinion polls carried out nationally in Ireland,[41] Britain[42] and Australia,[48] came up with very similar findings—even though different questions were asked.

In the Irish poll, nine per cent of people described themselves as 'constantly' in contact with a mentally handicapped person and 43 per cent as 'never' in contact. The comparable figures for our samples were eight per cent and 45 per cent.

In Britain, the poll did not enquire into frequency of contact but they did discover that 52 per cent 'did not know anyone who is mentally handicapped'. Likewise in Australia and Ireland, 54 per cent and 59 per cent respectively of those interviewed nationally had little or no contact with disabled people. (The figure was 52 per cent in our survey.)

Thus, for the majority of people in our society, their information about mental handicap is second- and third-hand. To rephrase a popular 30s song, they've danced with a man who's danced with a girl who's danced . . . not with the Prince of Wales but with a person who is mentally handicapped.

It is not surprising that the dancers on the periphery of the dance floor of handicap are misinformed, uncaring and apprehensive. Here's what some of our people had to say:

> *People don't have enough contact with them (mentally handicapped) —should be more—stigma attached—hidden fear.* Woman (40s).
>
> *Fear is the biggest problem. Mentally handicapped are stigmatised.* Man (40s).
>
> *People are afraid of the mentally handicapped for fear of doing the wrong thing. Not enough publicity.* Woman (20s).
>
> *I give help willingly—especially children—I've some experience of them. I was frightened at first but got used to it and made friends with them.* Woman (40s).
>
> *I'd like to get to know them but I'd want somebody with me.* Female teenager.

HOW PEOPLE COME INTO CONTACT WITH MENTAL HANDICAP

What brings people into contact with mental handicap? Past studies, such as the Mencap[42] poll in Britain, suggested that most contacts are made through families, friends and neighbours. Was this true for the people in our communities? We presented them with seven alternatives (see Figure below). If they answered 'yes', e.g. they said they had a mentally handicapped relative, we went on to ask if they had met them during the *past week*, *past year* or at some *other* time. We could then see whether this contact featured in their present lifestyle or was it something that was part of the past. (Needless to say, this question was omitted with the 45 per cent of people who said they had no contact with mentally handicapped adults. To save confusion we have calculated the results over *all* the people in the study, rather than as a percentage of those reporting contact.)

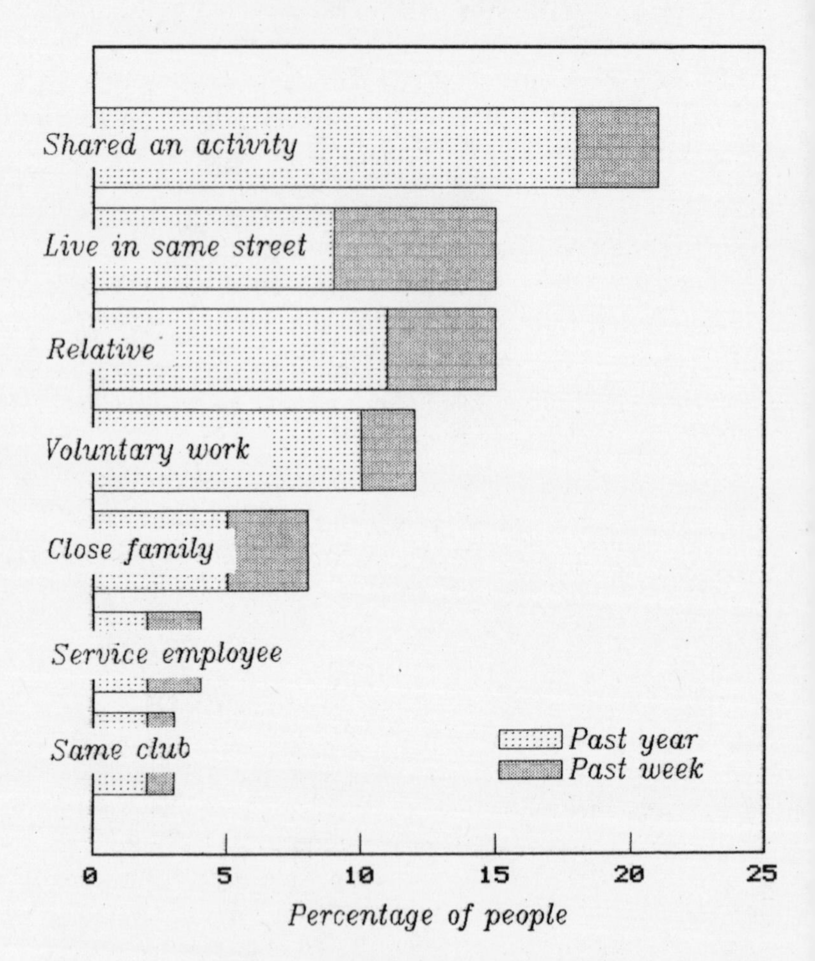

Range of contacts—As you can see, the most frequently reported way for people to come into contact with a mentally handicapped person was through sharing an activity with them. We did not ask people to give an example of what they did together, but if other findings are used as a guide this could cover anything from sitting beside one another on the bus, to spending a week as a voluntary helper at a camp for mentally handicapped people. Overall, about one in five people claimed to have 'shared' an activity with a mentally handicapped person.

We were more specific in the other alternatives we gave people. Notice how the percentage of people drops over the range of items. You must remember, too, that people could come into contact in more than one way, for example by doing voluntary work as well as having a disabled relative. In fact 14 per cent of our people did report two or more different ways of making contact, and a further 18 per cent reported one type of contact. Thus, in total, fewer than one third of the people we interviewed had ever experienced any of the contacts listed.

JUST OVER ONE IN 20 PEOPLE REPORTED CONTACTS WITHIN THE PAST WEEK

Weekly contacts were rare; most came through living in the same street as a mentally handicapped person or through having a relative who was mentally handicapped.

Implications—Regular contacts between disabled and non-disabled people are most likely to come about through families or by living in the neighbourhood. These findings confirm what has long been believed, namely that the community will only get to know mentally handicapped people if they remain part of that community. But what we may not have realised is how little impact these two forms of contact make on people in general—at least in terms of the number of non-handicapped people who have met and talked to a disabled peer; only one in ten at best.

It is unlikely that community awareness of mentally handicapped people will be boosted significantly merely by having them living in the community

Indeed this was vividly illustrated in our survey. We would call at a house to interview a young man and discover that he had a mentally handicapped brother living in the house with the family. Further down that road, we would ask the next person, 'Have you come across any mentally handicapped people who live in the same street as you?' and the answer was a definite NO. By the time we got to the end of the road, we might have heard that answer five times. People do not always know if there are mentally handicapped adults living in their locality. Some results still to come will reinforce this point even more.

In part, the solution is to have handicapped people more actively involved in community life. Surveys of their lifestyles in several countries[35, 50, 51] show a preponderance of home and family-based pursuits; only a minority go regularly to community recreational facilities—dances, pubs and clubs. If more were encouraged to join in, then more contacts might be made. Recall that nearly three per cent of the people in our study made contact through clubs.

A complementary approach is for the community to take the initiative rather than being left to respond to the presence of handicapped people in their midst. Our findings are encouraging in this regard. Over one in ten of our people have some experience of doing voluntary work, even if only one in 50 are presently involved. But results discussed in Chapters 7, 8 and 9 show that these are the very people who are most interested in knowing more about mental handicap and who are the most receptive to further contacts. They are a resource which can be built upon.

Some members of the public had their own ideas:

Not enough being done for mentally handicapped people in this area. They're hid away; people are ashamed to bring them out because of the way people look at them. Like to see them mixing more with normal children. I'd say there is a lot out here you don't hear about. Woman (40s).

Should be more suitable places for handicapped people, more sports facilities for them. Male Teenager.

More things in area for these type of people—more for everyone—social gatherings. Nothing in the area. Woman (50s).

Numbers of mentally handicapped people in the community

Although we may bemoan the lack of contact which the public has with mental handicap, the fact is that there are not all that many people with mental handicaps around. Surveys in Ireland put the figure at one in 250 adults.[52] Thus in a neighbourhood—electoral ward—of 3,000 people, there are likely to be on average only 12 mentally handicapped adults living there.

Against that, the people who took part in our study had more opportunities than most Dubliners for coming into contact. The two areas were deliberately chosen because a service for mentally handicapped people was located in each. Could it be that having a service in the midst of the community made little or no difference? Did the people in the area even know of the centre's existence and the type of people who attended it? As you will read, it is as well we took nothing for granted.

WHO KNOWS ABOUT THE CENTRES FOR HANDICAPPED PEOPLE?

> OVER HALF DID NOT KNOW THE DAY CENTRE EXISTED

> ONLY ONE THIRD KNEW THE GROUP HOME *AND* THE PEOPLE LIVING THERE

It is said that one of the joys of research is discovering the unexpected. For us joy was hardly the word—a jolt to our complacency, more aptly. In St Michael's House we had prided ourselves on providing services within the community. Indeed, the organisation began with a group of concerned parents and friends who wanted facilities provided locally so that their handicapped son or daughter could continue to live at home. And although we were aware that many of our Centres were physically separated —for example, with high walls around them—in recent years we had been deliberately trying to 'normalise' our newer developments, such as in the two areas chosen for this study. Our Centres may have been in the community but it is clear they were not part of that community.

The questions asked—Depending on the area, we asked, 'Is there a centre/house for handicapped people in this neighbourhood?' This question came after we had enquired about general community facilities and activities so that people were hopefully 'tuned in' to reflecting about their neighbourhood. Moreover, this was the first question referring to disability, so they should not have guessed our interest in this topic; a necessary precaution in case we predisposed people to answering Yes, when in reality they were only guessing.

Three alternative answers were provided:

* No, there is not (a centre/house);
* Don't know;
* Yes there is.

It was at this point that the interview branched. We said no more about a local centre to those answering that there was none, or who were unsure, and went on instead to ask other questions (see Chapter 5).

But those who said they knew the Centre got a real grilling! We asked:

a *Whereabouts is it?*—We wanted to confirm that the centre they knew was the one we had in mind. If they named a different one we asked, 'Are there any others?' and repeated it if they named yet another centre. There were, however, no other centres in the immediate vicinity, although some people (around ten per cent) did name a centre several miles away without knowing of the one in their own neighbourhood.

If people identified our Centre/house we asked them two further questions:

b *What sort of handicapped people . . . (attend that Centre) (live in that house?)*—Their replies would let us know how familiar they were with the Centre and we might get some clues as to how they perceived the clients' disability, particularly as a proportion of people in both Centres were physically and mentally handicapped, whereas others looked to have no disability.

c *Thinking of the people . . . who attend the Centre/live in the house . . . what contact have you had? Have you . . .?*—Five alternatives were given so that we could determine both the form and frequency of their contacts; we shall give fuller details when we come to the results.

KNOWLEDGE OF THE CENTRES

Knew centre & people
Knew centre only
Didn't know centre

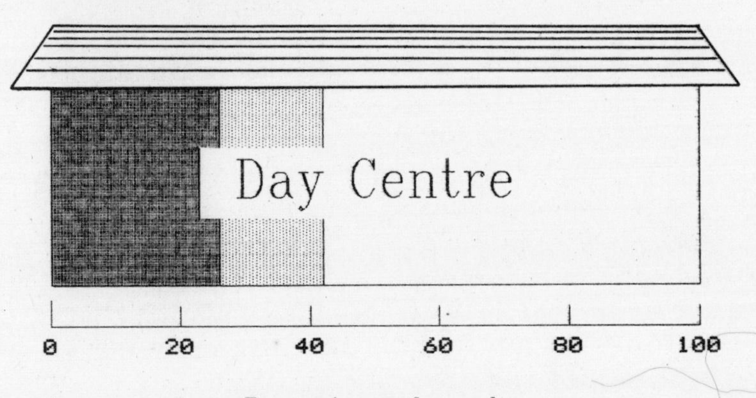

Percentage of people

Altogether, then, a pretty thorough cross-examination.

As you can see, just over one in three people, at best, knew that there was a service for *mentally handicapped* people in their neighbourhood. A rather surprising finding for us, as I have said, but at least we did have some warning while interviewing local people. It required some effort not to react when a person assured us that 'there's nothing for handicapped people within miles of this place', and just across the road from his house stood the Day Centre!

Overall, the Group Home was better known than the Day Centre—even if people were unsure as to the type of handicapped people who lived there (a theme we will take up in more detail in Chapter 5). A number of reasons might account for that, at the same time explaining why less than half the people in the other area did not know of the Day Centre.

Reasons for knowing:

* First, the Group Home had been opened seven years ago, whereas the Day Centre was only in its third year of operation. It looks as though it takes some years for a community to become aware of new services.
* Second, the houses used for the Group Home were on a corner site, close to a footpath leading from the housing estate to the shops and bus-stops, whereas the Day Centre occupied 'pre-fabs' at the rear of a primary school, the whole site being fenced off by railings. The accessibility of the site could be important for community contact.
* Third, residents in the Group Home were able to use shops and public transport or attend church without supervision, unlike the Centre attenders who were transported into and out of the area and only left the Centre on foot when they were accompanied by staff. The fact that there were ten times more day attenders than residents suggests that size is not always a pertinent factor, rather it is the client's 'profile' within the district.

* Fourth, the residents in the Group Home lived in that community: they were there in the evenings and at weekends; most left on public transport for work (sheltered employment) in the morning and returned with other workers in the late afternoon. The day attenders were the opposite. They came into the areas on weekdays only—around 10.00 a.m., leaving around 4.30 p.m. for home, where they spent their Saturdays, Sundays and holidays. Visitors to a neighbourhood may well go unnoticed.

Any one of these reasons, but more likely a combination of some of them, could explain the different levels of awareness in these two communities. We may get an idea of which ones are particularly crucial by looking at contacts between the community and people from the Centre, and the characteristics of the locals who have contact with the services. Let's see what these analyses throw up.

CONTACTS BETWEEN THE COMMUNITY AND HANDICAPPED PEOPLE FROM THE CENTRES

We could think of four types of contact which the community might have had with people from the Centres:

* Seen them walking around the neighbourhood (or, in the case of the Day Centre, they might also have seen them on their buses).
* Talked to them outside the Centre/house.
* Met them in the Centre/house.
* Invited them into my home.

We decided to check out all these alternatives with everyone who said they knew of the Centre or Group Home, but we also asked if they had any other contacts which we had not mentioned. Only two people gave instances: one knew the son of a friend who attended the Centre, and the second, a woman, went to Superslim classes at night-time in the Day Centre buildings. Hence

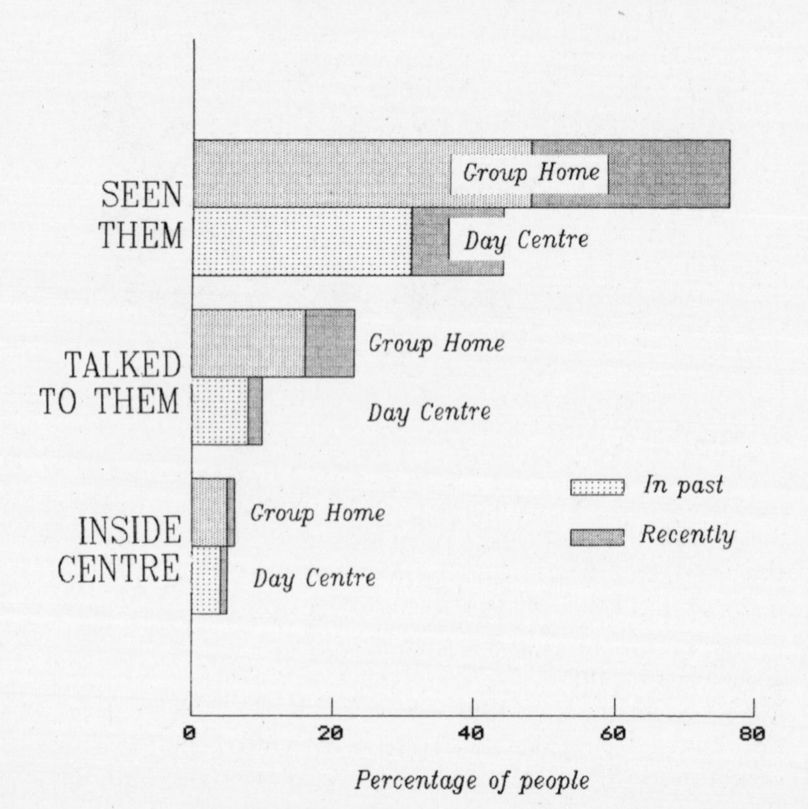

our alternatives more or less covered all the possibilities.

Type of contact is one important variable; frequency of contact is another. Hence we went on to ask if the contact had occurred in the past week, the past year or at some time earlier. The Figure gives the results for both type and frequency of contacts but I have omitted the results for 'invited the mentally handicapped person to my home', because in each area only three people had done this—two in one area and one in the other—and in all instances it had happened in the past. I recall one lady saying that a member of staff was delivering Christmas cards and had a handicapped person with her.

More than three-quarters of the people living in the area of the Group Home had seen the handicapped residents, compared to less than half of those living in the neighbourhood of the Day Centre.

A similar pattern was found when it came to talking to a mentally handicapped person, although the figures were very much lower—about a quarter of the people in the locality of the Group Home and only one in ten of the people in the area of the Day Centre.

In both areas, however, the extent to which local people came into the Centre or house was much the same—no more than one in 20. This was exactly the same percentage as reported in a London neighbourhood study[43] of community contacts with a hostel for 14 residents. They also found that only two per cent of people had been visited at home by one of the mentally handicapped residents.

The amount of recent contact in our study was depressingly low. It was most likely that about one in four people would have seen people from the Group Home in the neighbourhood, whereas in the Day Centre area at best only one in eight people would have seen the clients, usually going to and fro in their buses.

If the community does not come to the service, then it is even more crucial that the clients are out and about among the community. This happened much more frequently in the area with the Group Home, and—even though the total number of disabled people was only seven—the neighbours in that district were more familiar with both the service and the people and were more likely to have had contact during the previous week.

Perhaps there is a message here, too, for the way our services operate in the community. A woman in her 50s expressed it well when she said:

> *(They) don't give people much chance to be involved. Nobody comes to the door about it. Same with old residents—if called to give a meal or put to bed, I would lend a hand.*

WHO HAS BEEN IN CONTACT?

It is not enough to discover that some people know of the mental handicap service in their area whereas others do not. Rather we need information on the type of people who know. Once again we asked the computer to tell us who were the people in each community most likely to have had contact with the service and the clients. Here is the profile which emerged, *in order of importance.*

Women rather than men—44 per cent of women had contact as opposed to 32 per cent of men.

Knew more families in the locality—People who said they knew 16+ families in the area were the most likely to have had contact; 46 per cent compared to 26 per cent of those who knew only one or two families. Remember this variable came up before in contacts with handicapped people in general.

Allied to this were two other indicators: the people knowing the service had lived in the area for at least six years and they participated in two or more activities in that locality. Thus people who are settled within their community and most active within it are, not surprisingly, the ones most likely to know what is going on there.

Past contact with other mentally handicapped people—People who have come into contact with mental handicap in other spheres of their lives (as described earlier) are more likely to have contacts with the local centre.

30–49 years of age—This age group reported more contacts than did younger or older people.

By contrast, if a service is eager to make itself known to *all* the people in a locality, then these are the people who require particular attention:

* Males.
* People who know few families in the area; who are newly arrived, etc.
* Those who have had no past contact with mentally handicapped people.
* Teenagers, twenty-year-olds and the over 50s.

There were other factors which could reasonably be presumed to affect contact with the Centre or Group Home but which did not show up as significant in our analyses. For instance, we thought that people living closest to the Centre or house would be more likely to know of the Centre or to have contact with people from it. In fact when we checked this out, by comparing the replies of those living closest, with those living further away, there were no significant differences.

The same applied to people working or studying in the area, as opposed to those who travelled to other parts of the city. Either of these factors, however, could prove important in other localities.

One factor we could not explore was urban-rural differences. However, the study carried out in small towns in the west of Ireland[44] reported twice the number of people knowing of the local mental handicap centre (66 per cent versus 32 per cent in our Dublin study), and the smaller the town, the higher the percentage of people who knew of the centre.

IMPLICATIONS

Community-based services are now in vogue but the message from these figures is clear. Merely siting a service in a neighbourhood—particularly a city suburb—is no guarantee of interaction with the community or that local people will be aware of its existence. Paradoxically, staff in the service may have little perception of their isolation. The contacts they have with local people may be selective and sufficient to meet their expectations. Impressions about community contacts are not always accurate, as we discovered.

A fundamental question remains: do we want to publicise the service or, more particularly, that its clients are mentally handicapped? This issue will come up again in Chapter 5 but at this point we shall assume that it is good to let local people know about the service and what it is trying to do. Given our results, what is the best way of doing this? The following guidelines emerge:

Regular usage of community facilities by mentally handicapped people

This will include shops, cafés, swimming pools, etc., as well as more participation in activities such as evening classes, church groups, clubs, etc. It goes without saying that the handicapped people must cope successfully in these settings. Any bizarre or inappropriate behaviours will put people off and heighten their anxieties.

The key words are training and supervision. Handicapped people can learn to use community facilities but this must feature in the curriculum of their service. And they must have practice in real-life settings. Looking at pictures in the special centre, chatting with staff or even rôle-playing, are no substitute for the real thing.

Supervision, ideally on a one-to-one basis, is essential in the learning phase. Community helpers could make a valuable contribution here.

Identify active communities

Community involvement is more likely to come about in areas where there is a settled population and a range of resources in the area used by the local people. If you are in the luxurious position of being able to choose a location for a new service, you might bear those criteria in mind.

The less fortunate—i.e. most of us—would have to look for such sub-groups within the areas where our services were located. Identifying 'social networks' is the jargon term, but the reality is knowing who are the community activists in your area—clergy, residents' associations, leaders in youth organisations, for example. The people vary but the idea is the same. By building links with them you can reach out to the other people more speedily and effectively through using their networks.

To help in your detective work, here are some clues as to who is most likely to receive you kindly—30–49-year-old women who have lived in the area for at least six years and who have had some previous contact with mentally handicapped people. They are not the only ones, of course, but our guess is that you will find it more difficult to interest 20-year-old males who are lodging in the district, in anything like the same numbers . . . unless you make a particular effort to attract them.

Create a community spirit

The reality of modern urban life is that communities exist as geographical locations rather than as social entities. In such settings, the potential for community involvement is dramatically reduced as people commute out of the area for both work and entertainment or retreat into their homes to watch television or videos. There is little a mental handicap service can do to stem this tide—on its own. But by linking with other agencies involved in community development, the task becomes more manageable. That is one idea. Another is to share 'ownership' of the service with people in that area. Three simple questions will illustrate the point:

* Are the clients from the locality?
* Do the staff of the service come from or live in that neighbourhood?
* Are the 'managers' of the service local people?

If the answer is *no* to all three, how can that service be

called a community service? Which community is it serving? Might it be that the arbitrary development of so-called 'community' services in localities could contribute to the breaking up of a community identity?

5 Who Do They Think They Are?

People think we're all the same—but we're not all the same; we're not all the same.

Dublin woman working in sheltered employment

Mental handicap is a puzzling condition to the professional and layperson alike. It has been around for centuries, yet its defining features—low intelligence accompanied by poor social competence—were only spelt out in the 1900s and agreed internationally as late as the 1950s.

To those professionally involved with mentally handicapped people, the diagnosis of this condition appears relatively straightforward. Some may even pride themselves on recognising mentally handicapped people 'a mile off'. However, simply labelling a person—even when accurately done and with the full panoply of multi-disciplinary assessments—still does not explain the condition. If anything, professional wisdom has made it even harder for the proverbial man or woman in the street to understand this phenomenon. Here are three examples of what I mean.

CHANGES

Firstly, every twenty years or so, the name of this condition has been changed . . . mental deficiency . . . mental subnormality . . . mental retardation . . . slow learner . . . severe learning difficulties, etc. Of course, you cannot argue with the rationale for these changes, but the unfortunate side-effect is a confused public who are left wondering what the differences are between them. Or as one man said to me in all seriousness, 'You know this thing you call Down Syndrome, is there such a thing as an Up Syndrome?' His son was what used to be called a mongol.

Secondly, a generation ago, the 'right thing' to do with mentally handicapped children was to have them placed in full-time care, away from their families. Today's professionals have done a complete U-turn, and while they may now condemn their predecessors' recommendations, those members of the public who still think it is best if 'they are put away', can hardly be blamed when it is we who have changed our minds.

Third, tremendous energy is expended in persuading people to dip into their pockets to help the mentally handicapped—'people who can't help themselves' or, in the words of the famous, or infamous, Mencap poster campaign of a few years back, 'Some families have a cross to bear this Christmas'. These messages go out alongside admonitions to 'treat them as you would any other person', or appeals for the community to get involved in their care. As the North American Indians so graphically expressed it, 'White man speak with forked tongue!'

MENTAL HANDICAP IS JUST ANOTHER DISABILITY

Public confusion about mental handicap is further fuelled

by the presumption that it is just another disability. Professional knowledge has long since dispelled such simplistic notions. For example:

* **The mentally handicapped are all the same.** *WRONG!* The term mental handicap covers a whole range of conditions whose outcomes are broadly similar in that the person shows developmental delays, but the diversity among people labelled mentally handicapped is very much greater than that found among those afflicted by poor hearing or loss of sight.

Mental handicap is best thought of as an umbrella term for a whole range of conditions.

* **The mentally handicapped look different.** *WRONG!* Some may have obvious deformities but not all do. You can find children who look physically normal in services for the most severely handicapped, whereas others with peculiar features—such as those with Down's Syndrome—can be nominated for a place at their local ordinary school.

Mental handicap is determined by *behavioural* rather than *physical* criteria.

* **Once mentally handicapped, always mentally handicapped.** *WRONG AGAIN!* The division between mental handicap and normality is not at all clear-cut. Given support and training, the handicapped person could become as socially competent as his or her peers. Some may marry, hold down a job or run a home of their own.

Likewise, people can move between the sub-categories of the condition—severely handicapped people can be reclassed as moderately handicapped, for instance. Sadly, some of our service systems, notably in education, have been slow to recognise this fact.

All in all, the term 'mental handicap' is not easily explained. In essence, it would be better described as a *developmental* disability; the consequence being slowed-down development and slower learning rates, but this can vary from marginal to exceptional. Yet how many people have got this message? We wanted to find out, so we asked our people, *'What do the words mental handicap mean to you?'*

Some of you may feel that this question would not be out of place in the final degree papers for university students, and I suspect some of our interviewees thought likewise. I would swear that a few of them visibly paled at that point in the interview.

But our concern was not to make them sweat or even to test whether they knew the 'right' answer. Rather we wanted to have some insight into the images which these words conjured up for them. What misconceptions did they have? . . . what other handicaps did they confuse it with? . . . who were the people most likely to know the essential features of this disability? To do this exhaustively would of course require a very different approach from the one we used, such as an in-depth interview by a cosy fireside, rather than a doorstep interrogation on a winter's evening.

Instead, we opted for the 'first thoughts' technique which also has a venerable history in psychological research. The rationale is that by catching people unawares, they are less likely to give defensive or socially acceptable answers. You tap the thoughts or associations which come most readily to mind.

However, after the person had responded to the question, 'What do the words mental handicap mean to you?', we added a 'probe'—'Anything else you want to add?' Probes are commonly used in interviews, especially with so-called 'open questions'. The more complex the topic you are inviting people to talk about, the more essential it is to include a probe. Otherwise, you run the risk of oversimplifying or misinterpreting their responses.

Once you decide to include a probe, however, it must be used with every person you interview, no matter how verbose their initial response has been. The converse is also true: you cannot start using probes half-way through the study.

THE ANSWERS

ONLY ONE IN FOUR PEOPLE KNEW STRAIGHT AWAY THE KEY FEATURE OF MENTAL HANDICAP

As you have probably guessed, if you ask 419 people about what mental handicap means to them, you can get about 419 different answers. As I shall explain later, we had to group people's replies, but even so, only one quarter came up with any reference to 'slowness' or retarded development in their first response to the question, and less than half made any mention in their reply.

But we were just as interested in people's misconceptions and confusions and, like many an open question, this one, too, yielded a rich harvest. Our selection ranged from almost textbook definitions of mental handicap to very esoteric replies including—'No IQ'; 'Make you realise the blessings you have'; 'Social disorder' and 'Poison'. The last comment came from an elderly gentleman who once lived next door to a family with a mentally handicapped teenager. This boy persistently threw things over the wall, causing damage to the man's property and, when he complained, the parents abused him. Hence he summed up his feelings in one word—poison.

I was told all this sitting in the family living-room with the embarrassed wife trying to get her husband to shut up and admonishing me for writing it all down. Her attitude was that you cannot tar everyone with the same brush and that it was all in the past anyway. But the more she said, the more her husband went on to recount further 'horror' stories. I had visions of a full-scale row developing which I valiantly tried to defuse by working through the remaining questions. I think peace had been restored before I left, but it was an object lesson for me as to how markedly different perceptions can co-exist within the same family.

Grouping the replies—The wealth of data generated by

open questions is not readily amenable to computer analysis. The chief way of coping is to group people's replies into discrete categories which reflect a common theme. For example, we read through all the replies we had been given to this question and then drew up a tentative categorisation. We tested this by going through the questionnaires once again to get an idea of the relative size of each category and assess whether all responses were being covered. Adaptations were made as necessary before we embarked upon the final coding. At this stage we had upwards of 30 categories, but these were later regrouped as follows:

Slow/Backward/Immature—This category embraced responses such as 'delayed'; 'not as quick as other people'; 'don't have same understanding' and 'never grow up'.

Different—Other people conveyed a sense of mentally handicapped people being different but they did not spell out in what way, viz. 'they're disabled', 'brain-damaged', 'abnormal' and 'different degrees of it'.

Other disability—In some instances people appeared to define mental handicap in terms of associated problems or else confuse it with another handicap. Examples would be 'psychologically ill', 'in wheelchair', 'can't speak' or 'crippled'.

Alternative name—Here people merely used a synonym for mental handicap, such as 'mentally retarded' (by far the most popular), 'mentally deficient', 'mongol' and 'Down's Syndrome'.

Positive attitude—Sometimes people's comments conveyed an attitude rather than a definition: for instance, 'no different from us', 'cheerful, happy people', 'you'd feel sorry for them', 'a person, not freaks'.

Negative attitude—By contrast, other people conveyed a more negative attitude, viz. 'mad', 'burden', 'violent' or 'poison'.

Don't know or no response—Some people were literally lost

for words, such as one gentleman who hmm'd and ha'd for what seemed like ages then asked if he could come back to that question. When, to his surprise, I did, he still did not have an answer. We ended up agreeing that 'yes, it was a difficult one!'

In a few instances it was hard to decide into which category people's responses should go—'No IQ', for example: could that imply a negative attitude? In fact we opted to include it in the *'different'* category. In general, though, this was a minor problem.

POPULARITY OF RESPONSES

What, then, were the most popular perceptions of mental handicap among our people? We calculated two indexes of popularity:

a For each person's *first* mentioned comment.

b For *any* mention of this category, in that people could give two different ideas, especially after the probe 'Anything else you want to add?' was used. (Incidentally, these percentages will exceed 100 as people will be counted in two or more categories.)

As you can see, the overall pattern is the same in either case, but nearly everyone took advantage of the opportunity to say more, except in the case of explicitly negative comments, which were first-mentions.

Top of the poll were what might be called 'right' responses, but what is not so satisfying is the low percentage of people overall who correctly identified the key feature of this disability. At best, it gets to about half. Most people give another name, candidly state they don't know, mention that they are different in some way or, worse still, confuse them with another disability.

Our results broadly confirm the findings reported for the London neighbourhood survey[43] which used a very similar question, 'If I said someone was mentally handicapped, what would that mean to you?' They credited 57 per cent of people interviewed with a 'clear definition' of

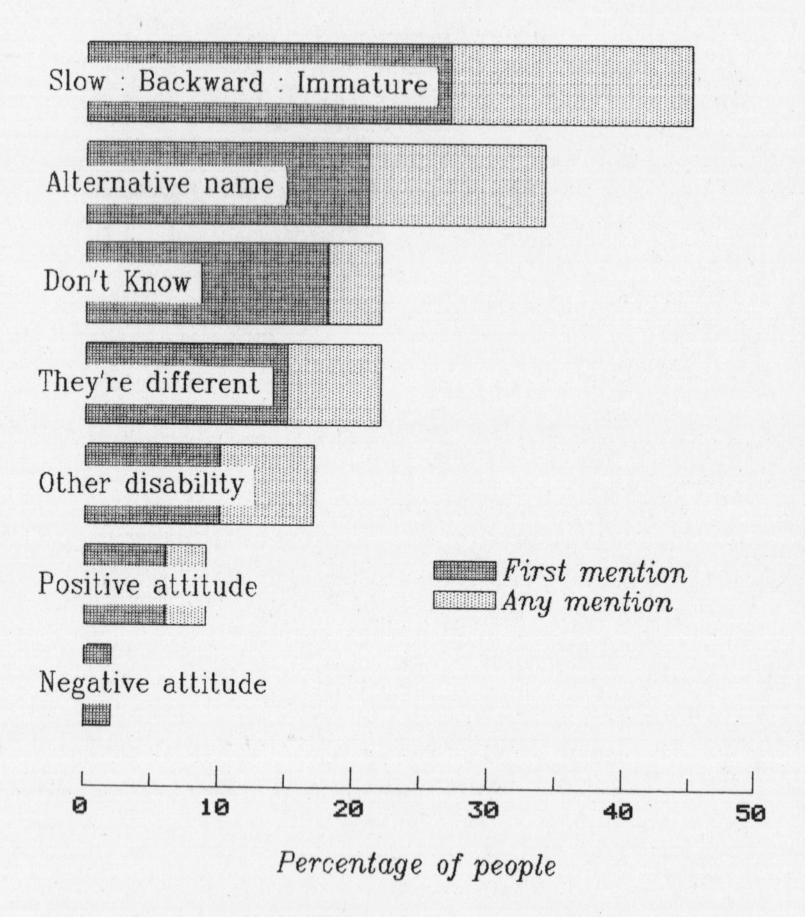

the term (45 per cent in Dublin); 14 per cent as confusing it with another disability (17 per cent in Dublin) and 18 per cent as 'Don't knows' (22 per cent in Dublin).

All of this bears out many of the points made at the beginning of the chapter. The public do *not* have a clear picture of this disability. Here are the views of four Dubliners:

What kind of handicap do you mean? Really handicapped like can't talk or walk? There's two on the bus in the mornings—very chatty and friendly. There's others that I'd be afraid of, who can't talk very well. Female teenager.

A mentally handicapped person gets a slagging when he comes on the bus. Blokes make fun; it's hard not to laugh when mickey taken but others tell them to stop. If very slow, won't call him mentally retarded. Male teenager.

I find it a very delicate subject to bring up and talk about. Man (30s).

We don't really know very much about it—it's very hard to talk about it. Woman (20s).

In terms of attitudinal statements made, it is encouraging that the positive comments—'cheerful, happy people'—far outweighed the negative ones. And as this was the first question about mental handicap, they should not have been biased by our interest in this topic.

A recent American study[33] with college students found that they, too, rated mentally handicapped people as more 'loving', 'honest', 'forgiving' and 'cheerful' than they did 'persons of "normal" intelligence'. The author rightly concluded that this was 'a much more positive perception of these persons than has generally been reported in the literature.'

However, it is possible that people we interviewed felt more negatively than they were prepared to admit—a point we'll take up again later on when reviewing the results of their reactions to having mentally handicapped people living next door as neighbours (Chapter 7).

Meanwhile, here's a flavour of the variety in their comments:

They don't need anything, just food and bed; they should be done away with at birth. Woman (60s).

They should have more scope—they're just ordinary human beings like everybody else. Woman (40s).

If I had the time I'd like to know more about them and any mental disorder. We've all some sort of quirk. Man (40s).

WHO'S LIKELY TO BE RIGHT?

How come some people give a right definition and others do not? What makes the difference? You could probably predict which people are the most likely to give a 'right' response, but rather than rely on your guesses—or mine—I'll tell you who they were in our sample.

For a start, some of the likely predictors, such as age, sex and social background, were not significant. (The Mencap poll[42] in Britain suggested that women had more favourable perceptions than men; that younger people had a more positive impression than their elders and that people from higher social classes were also more aware of likely problems, yet still positive in their outlook.) Instead, the big difference in our survey—and also found in the Mencap poll—was whether or not the person had met disabled

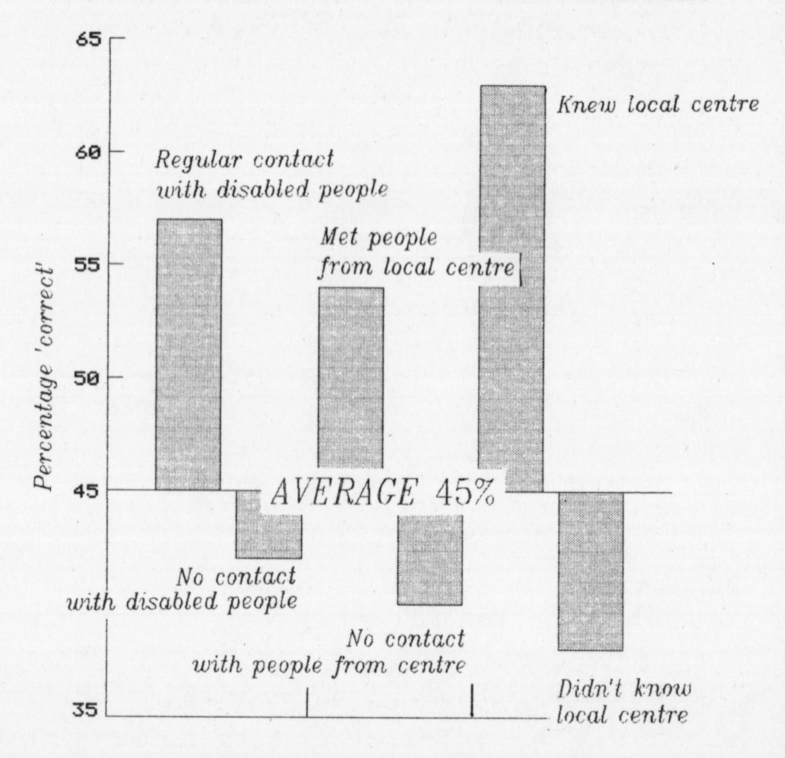

people in general or, more particularly, the mentally handicapped people who attended the local Centre.

As the Figure shows, significantly more than the average number of people were able to define mental handicap in terms of 'slowness' if they had regular contact with disabled people or if they had met—even just seen—the people from the Centre (see Chapter 4).

Moreover, the people who could define mental handicap 'correctly' were the ones who were most likely to know that the local Centre was for *mentally handicapped* people.

The problem—as with the chicken and the egg—is which came first? Perhaps they recognised the people from the local Centre because they knew the characteristics of mental handicap as opposed to other disabilities. But equally it could be that it was the people from the local Centre who 'taught them' what it means to be mentally handicapped.

One of my favourite proverbs is, 'The things we know best are the things we have not been taught', the implication being that our personal experience and problem-solving teaches us so much. More textbooks, talks or television programmes may—just may—give the public a better understanding of mental handicap. I suspect that people are more likely to learn if they can discover its essential attributes through meeting people.

WHO ATTENDS THE LOCAL CENTRE?

But let us come back to the public's perceptions of the people who attended the local Centre. You will recall from Chapter 4 that only two in five people knew of the Day Centre's existence, whereas nearly eight out of nine knew about the Group Home. But as the Figure below shows, the proportion of people in each area who knew that the centres were for mentally handicapped people were not all that different. Many people, especially in the area of the Group Home, were not able to say who attended, or else they thought it was for some other disabled group. Among those mentioned were: physically disabled, epileptic, autistic,

WHO ATTENDS THE LOCAL CENTRE?

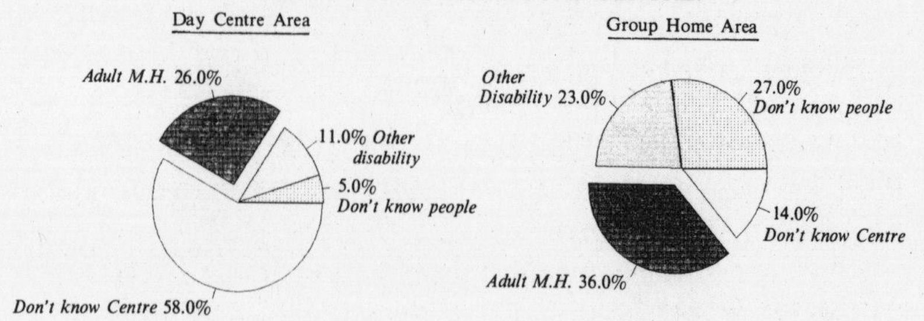

multiple sclerosis, blind, spina bifida, old folks or, as one person phrased it, 'those who have gone altogether'.

In a sense, some of these confusions are understandable. There were people in both centres who fitted some of these descriptions—an instance of when a little knowledge can be a dangerous thing. But then again, as our analyses showed, the people most likely to know that the Centre was for *mentally handicapped adults* were those who had seen or met people from the Centre. Once again, this was the dominant discriminator although other variables also contributed, most notably sex (females rather than males) and, somewhat puzzlingly, length of schooling (those finishing at 15 were more likely to know that mentally handicapped people attended than were those who continued on at school until 18 years, or who had taken tertiary level education).

By and large these results are much the same as those reported earlier, even though we have narrowed the reference from the abstract phrase 'mental handicap' to a specific group of handicapped people in each area, who were known by at least three-fifths of all the persons we interviewed. Even then, at best just about one third of the public recognised the characteristics of mental handicap.

EXPLAINING MENTAL HANDICAP

The results present us with a quandary, however. Do we want everyone to know that a centre is for people who are mentally handicapped? If we did, then we could plaster signs all over the Centre saying that it is for 'the mentally handicapped'. This goes against much of the normalisation philosophy and we had no signs on either of our Centres. But even if signs were used, there is no guarantee that people would have any greater understanding of what it means to be mentally handicapped.

Yet if we do not make clear who is attending the Centre and why they are there, we run the risk of leaving uncorrected some of the public's misunderstandings of this disability, or allowing 'misinformation' to circulate.

We can get some clues for possible actions from the results we have obtained.

Personal contact—Above all else, personal contact is likely to be the most effective way of making people more aware of what it means to be mentally handicapped. Meeting a range of mentally handicapped people from a local centre is the ideal, but even talking to one person may suffice.

It's likely, too, that the average man or woman in the street will find it more informative to talk with a member of staff or parent about the effects of being mentally handicapped, rather than being given leaflets or newspaper articles to read.

Diversity—The term mental handicap should not be used in an unqualified way. For instance, it must be stressed that there are different degrees of this disability (mild, moderate, severe); that people can have additional disabilities (some are mentally and physically disabled; others may have epilepsy as well as mental handicap), and that mental handicap may result from different conditions—Down's Syndrome, cerebral palsy and so forth.

Slowness—The core of this disability is 'slowed-down' development. This emphasis is best conveyed by terms such as 'developmental delay' or 'slow learner'. Interestingly, these are the names most preferred by many parents of handicapped children.[53] Such terms also avoid the unfortunate connotations of the word 'mental' and confusion with mental illness, a common mistake especially among teenagers.

They are people, too—Finally, the human-ness of the disabled people can be stressed by emphasising what they can do as well as what they cannot; by referring to feelings and social relations as well as intellectual skills, and by giving the public opportunities to see and meet handicapped people in a range of settings—at work, at rest and at play.

Our goal is simply stated. It is to demystify mental handicap. The days when people were shut away in institutions far removed from their families and neighbours are drawing to a close. People today need to know. They may sit beside a mentally handicapped person on the bus as they go to work, they will see them at the swimming baths, cinema and cafés, and some will live next door to them. As one teenager whom we interviewed put it, '*If we knew more about mental handicap, we'd be better able to cope*'.

Labelling people, it is argued, does them a disservice.[54] But there is also a sense in which it has been a disservice to the public, too. Their perceptions of these people are often fossilised by myths, half-remembered facts and inaccurate associations all triggered by the words 'mentally handicapped'. Changing the name of the condition is not the solution. Rather people need to perceive the person and react to that, rather than to a label. The best way of doing that is through coming into contact with disabled people. But do people in the community want this to happen? That is the theme of the next chapter.

6 Who's Prepared to Meet Mentally Handicapped People?

> I need a friendship; I wish I had a companion, a boy I could have as a companion, that I could go out with and chat to. I have nobody and it hurts me.
>
> *Young adult living at home with ageing parents*

Integrating handicapped people into community life, if it means anything, will involve them in meeting many different people in their locality and beyond. People with disabilities may be prepared to do this, but are their neighbours? In this chapter you will get the answers to that question and associated ones, such as:

* How confident are people at the prospect of meeting a person who is mentally handicapped?
* What sort of contacts are people prepared to accept and which ones do they consider are the most likely to occur?
* Who in the community are happy to meet mentally handicapped people and who would prefer to avoid doing so?

CONFIDENCE AT MEETING

Problem—how do you get people to confess their inadequacies to strangers? We certainly did not want to challenge people's self-esteem by asking, 'Have you the confidence to meet mentally handicapped people?' That is the sort of question to which nearly everyone would have to answer 'Yes'. Moreover the question gives few clues to the implications of the term 'confidence'. Much better to spell out precisely what you have in mind so that people can 'measure' themselves against a criterion. But there is still a problem. You have to define the reactions people might have. And how do you do that? . . . You ask them!

During the first phase of our research programme, we were mainly interested in teenagers' reactions to mental handicap and we explored their feelings about the prospect of meeting a person of roughly their own age who was mentally handicapped. We began by having seven different classes of fifth form students discussing their reactions. We kept notes on the feelings expressed. At the end we had listed more than 30 different reactions, among the more expressive were:

try to get away as quickly as possible
would not want to be seen
feel scared
find it a good experience.

At this stage we had no idea which reactions were the most common, but we went on to find out by showing the list to many more students (250 plus) and asking them to rate the extent to which each one applied to them. From those data we could then discover, by using a statistical technique called Factor Analysis,[40] not only the most common reactions, but also the overlap between reactions which embodied the same basic concept, even though they were worded differently. By now, the list had been whittled down to eight items and these were used in a questionnaire survey of young people's reactions, in which more than 1,400 students in the Irish Republic participated.[55]

Subsequently, many of these students took part in a school-based educational programme on mental handicap which involved meeting mentally handicapped peers from a local Centre. Teachers and pupils attested to the success of the programme and our measures of attitude change confirmed this.[56] The most dramatic improvement showed in the students' reactions to contact—as measured by the eight items. Subsequent analysis showed that four out of the eight items were particularly sensitive and it was these four which we used in the neighbourhood study discussed in this book, two years, 1,600 students and goodness knows how many reams of computer print-out later!

The question

We asked people to imagine that they were to meet a mentally handicapped person at their home. We gave four possible reactions, one at a time, viz:

'Would you . . .

feel embarrassed?
know what to say?
find it a good experience?
know how to react?'

For each reaction, we asked people to pick one of the five options which best described their feelings:

Definitely not
No
Unsure
Yes
Definitely yes

These five options were typed on a card which the interviewer showed people to help them choose—a standard interviewing procedure. It sounds cumbersome but it worked reasonably well.

The question was introduced as follows: 'If a friend brought a mentally handicapped person, whom you had never met before in your life, to your house tomorrow, would you . . .' Then came the four reactions, beginning with, 'feel embarrassed?' The person selected from the five options the one which described his feelings. Then came the next question: 'Would you know what to say?' to which the person gave an answer, and so on.

'Ah,' I hear you say, 'aren't you just measuring people's confidence in meeting other people? How do you know it's their reactions to *mentally handicapped* people that you're getting?' Good question. The answer, as any social researcher who wants to be kept in a job will tell you, is to ask another question.

That's what we did. We had people go through the same four reactions but this time thinking about their feelings 'if the friend brought a *stranger* who wasn't handicapped to your house'. We could then compare their answers and see if the description 'mentally handicapped' made a difference. Not surprisingly, it did.

But this confirmation was obtained at a price: interviewers and interviewees alike found it rather tedious to go through the same reactions and in fact we dropped the 'stranger' questions when we came to do the survey in the area of the Group Home.

Confidence scores

We transformed people's replies to the four items into a *confidence score*. The maximum score was 20 (five points per item multiplied by four items) and the minimum was four (one point per item multiplied by four items).

Five points were awarded for choosing 'definitely yes', four for 'yes', three for 'unsure', down to one for 'definitely not'. However, in the case of the item, 'feel embarrassed', the order was reversed: 'definitely not' scored five and 'definitely yes' scored one, so that confident people always got the higher scores.

If I tell you that the average score on this scale was 14.9 points, it will not mean a great deal to you, I know, except that it is some way off the top score of 20. However, that is not really the purpose of this measure—it is not intended to stand alone. These numbers only make sense when they are used in comparisons. If you like, it can help to accentuate the differences which might otherwise be overlooked. Some examples will make clearer what we mean.

On average, people had higher confidence scores for meeting a stranger than they did for meeting mentally handicapped people (15.7 *vs.* 14.9). The average difference may not be great, but what is significant is that many more people scored lower on meeting a mentally handicapped person compared to a stranger than vice versa, and it is this which forms the basis of statistical analysis.

Remember, too, that it is an *average* difference. For some people, the difference in scores was very much greater, although this would be compensated by others having no difference in scores.

WHO ARE THE MOST CONFIDENT?

The over 50s who have had regular contact with disabled people

In the main, people's confidence was affected by two factors: the extent of their past contacts with disabled people and their age. The results are shown below and, as you can see, there is a whopping difference of nearly five points between the top and bottom groups.

Interestingly, a similar analysis of scores for confidence in meeting a stranger yielded a different pattern of results. Age was still a factor—the older you are the more confidence you have—but linked with this was people's involvement in activities within the neighbourhood. Those involved in three or more pursuits scored on average three points higher than people involved in one or no activities (18.4 *vs.* 15.4). This is useful confirmation that the questions were valid—that is, measuring what they were designed to measure, namely people's confidence in meeting other people.

Measuring people's confidence in this way—useful as it is—is more appealing to the social researcher than to the service planner. Hence we went on to enquire about people's reactions to particular types of contact, all of which could happen to them if mentally handicapped people were to become more actively involved in community life. But as you will read, it often comes back to the person's level of confidence.

REACTIONS TO DIFFERENT SORTS OF CONTACT

They say one should not believe everything one sees in print; it is even truer for computer print-outs. I fear that

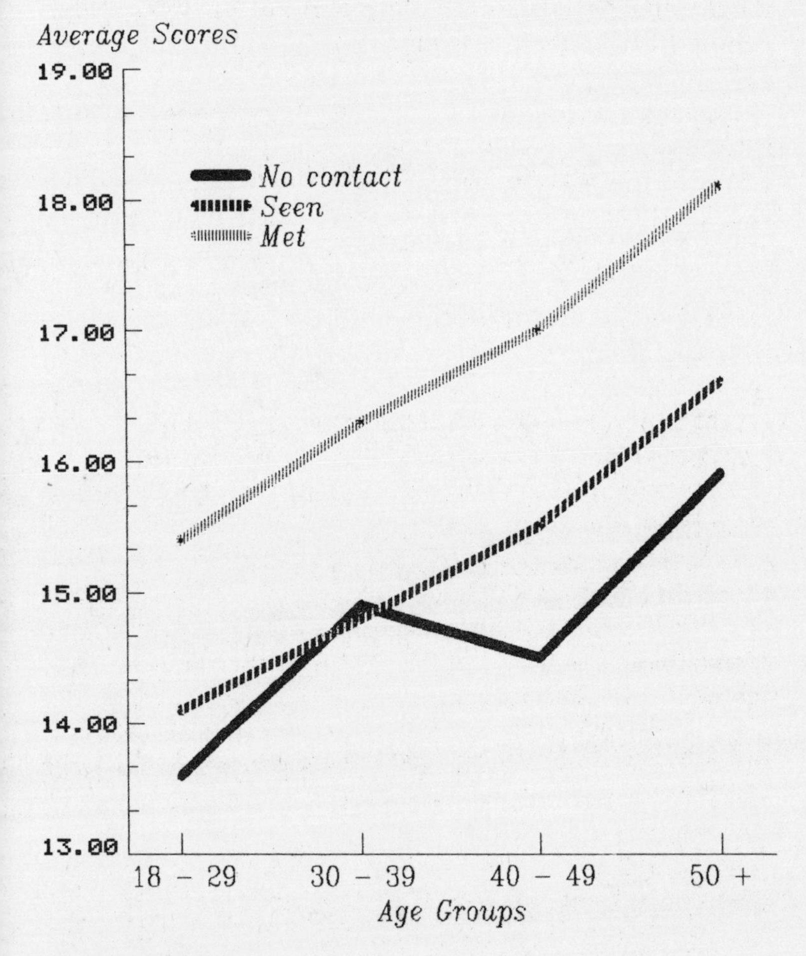

the results about people's reactions to contact with disabled people are often too good to be true. In the Irish National Poll,[41] for example, nearly three out of five people said they would 'accept completely' mentally handicapped people joining in their social activities. The small town study in the west of Ireland[44] reported phenomenally high 'approval' ratings—percentages were in the high 90s for having a mentally handicapped person from the local centre sit beside you in the pub, joining local clubs or befriending a member of the family. They balked somewhat at having a friend or family member dating a mentally handicapped person, but nonetheless, more than a third still approved.

Perhaps the Irish have very positive attitudes to social integration. But even the London neighbourhood survey[43] reported that 64 per cent of people were willing to have a mentally handicapped person as a visitor to their home and 83 per cent were prepared to work alongside one.

Sad to say, these figures do not square with reality. The problem with asking people to predict their reactions is that they may not behave in the way they said or thought they would. Social research is replete with examples of mismatches between intentions and actions—the most publicised being the apparent failure of opinion pollsters to predict the outcomes of general elections or referenda.

One reason for this, in our type of research, is that people tend to give socially acceptable answers rather than those which best describe their feelings. Hence, people may say they would encourage contact with mentally handicapped people so that the interviewer will think better of them, even if they have no intention of ever doing it. It is particularly easy for people to give this sort of answer if they believe there is little chance of them being put to the test. For instance, if they think there is little likelihood of their meeting a handicapped person in a café, they can safely say they would encourage that person to sit beside them, even though they know in their heart of hearts that they probably would not do so.

By contrast, a person who believes such contacts are likely to happen and still says he or she would encourage them, is a different type of character. We need some way of sorting them out from the others. I think we can modestly claim to have done it!

A new type of question

A favourite technique of researchers studying attitudes to minority groups is the Bogardus Social Distance Scale, named after its originator E.S. Bogardus, who first published the idea in 1924. It consists of a series of questions designed to explore people's tolerance for contact with the group in question. Early items involve little or no personal contact, e.g. 'would exclude (these people) from my country'; 'would allow as visitors to my country'; but later ones envisage an intimate relationship developing, e.g. 'admit to my club as personal chums' or 'to close kinship by marriage'.

We could have used Bogardus' original items in this investigation and treated our results much like our 'Confidence in Meeting' scale. Instead, we felt it would be more valuable to explore people's reactions to contacts which were likely to occur with mentally handicapped people in the community. We chose five items, arranged in order from low to high personal contact. The question began as follows:

'In daily life we are often "forced" to meet people. I would like to get your views on how you would feel if a mentally handicapped adult . . .' Then followed the five situations, one at a time:

'. . . said hello to you in the street;
'. . . sat beside you on a bus, train or in a café;
'. . . joined in your social activities;
'. . . wanted to become your friend;
'. . . if your best friend (or son/daughter, depending on age of person involved) wanted to marry a mentally handicapped adult'.

People could choose one of three options as their reply to each situation:

'I would prefer they didn't'.
'It would be OK with me'.
'I would encourage it'.

Thus we would be able to find out the percentage of people willing to encourage each type of contact. Or would we? We made a major modification to the traditional social distance scale to help ensure a more accurate picture.

'Is it likely to happen?'—We asked each person an additional question after they replied to the 'type of contact' question, namely, 'Do you think it's likely to happen?' Thus the sequence was as follows:

QUESTIONS	POSSIBLE ANSWERS
1 How would you feel if a mentally handicapped adult said hello to you in the street? Would you . . .	*Prefer they didn't/It would be OK with you/You would encourage it*
Do you think it's likely to happen?	*No/Yes/Unsure*
2 How would you feel if they sat beside you on a bus, train or in a café? Would you . . .	*Prefer they didn't/It would be OK by you/You would encourage it*
Do you think it's likely to happen?	*No/Yes/Unsure*

. . . and so we continued until all five types of contact were explored.

THE READY, WILLING AND UNABLE

Unlike past surveys, which tend to categorise people into two groups—those who 'approve' of more contact and those who disapprove—we were able to identify four groupings, whom we affectionately nicknamed Ready, Willing and Unable, along with a fourth, the Uncaring.

Ready—Those who think that contact is likely *and* they would encourage it.

> *Would like to see some joining in sports at school, e.g. basketball, football.* Male Teenager.

Willing—Those who do not think that contact is likely but they say they would encourage it.

Would love to see more integration but tough due to neighbourhood. Woman 40s.

Unable—Those who think that contact is likely but who would *not* encourage it.

Mentally handicapped I find I'm not comfortable with. Woman 30s.

Uncaring—These people do not feel that contact is likely and, anyway, they would not encourage it.

I won't go out of my way to meet people of any kind. Man 20s.

The PIE charts for each type of contact let you see the relative proportions of people meeting the above descriptions. There's a lot to take in and they may seem very

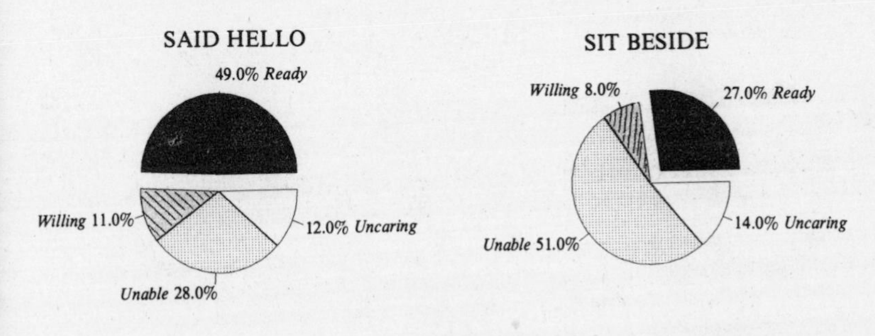

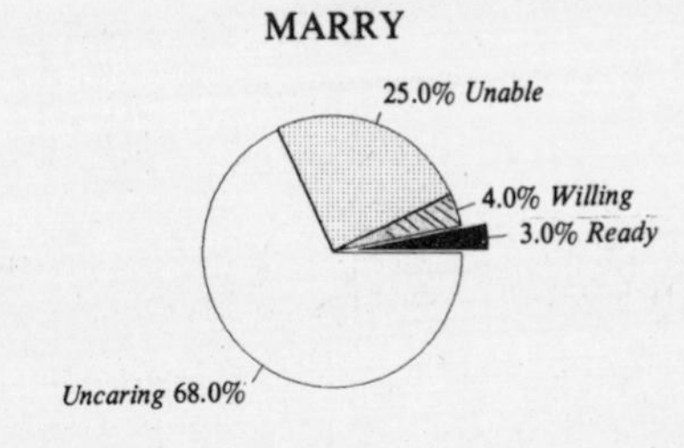

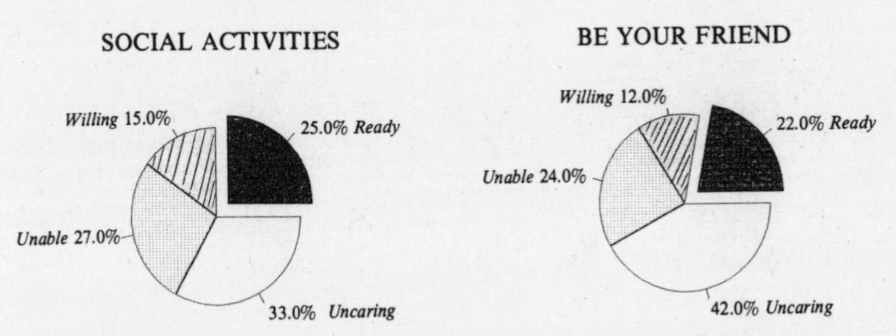

complicated, but the following pointers may guide you through them.

* Notice how the patterns change across the five items. This means that people react differently to the various forms of contact—they will tolerate some more than others. The first two—'say hello' and 'sit beside you'—get similar ratings, at least in terms of these being likely to happen (i.e. adding the percentages for the Readys and Unables). Items three and four—'join in social activities' and 'be your friend'—also form a pair, whereas item five, 'marriage', stands alone.
* The next feature to explore is how the sizes of the four groups of people change across the items. Let's begin with the Readys.

* **The Ready**

As you can see, on all items they number less than half, and on average only one in four people are ready for the social contacts implied in items two, three and four. This drops even further on item five but then, only a minority of parents or professionals are ready to contemplate the possibility of mentally handicapped people marrying.

* **The Willing**

They never number more than one in six people and significantly this proportion is reached on an item—'join social activities'—which gives lots of scope for socially acceptable answers, particularly if the person is not a socialite. So it looks as though our people were not ducking our questions too much. It may not require too much effort to persuade this group that contacts with disabled people are becoming more likely than ever before.

* The Unable

For me, this is the most interesting of all the groups—those who feel that contact is likely but they will not encourage it. The percentage of people varies greatly over the four items, peaking on item two—sitting beside a mentally handicapped person in a café, or on a bus or train—but one in four are reluctant to have social contacts (items three and four), even though they think they are likely. Maybe if these people were given a chance to meet some disabled people, they might change their attitude. We shall explore this possibility in a moment.

* The Uncaring

Our nickname might be unfair, but it is hard to think of a more suitable one—'apathetic' sounded too derogatory. Whatever we call them, I think that we can take heart that the number of people in this group is so small, at least on items one, two and three. Of course, it may be that some influential people within the community fall within this group—for instance, those who will actively oppose the opening of a Group Home in their neighbourhood. But then again, in a democracy, numbers also count and this group is in a minority on all contact items but the last.

IMPLICATIONS

Compared to previous surveys, our people appear reluctant to have contact with mentally handicapped people. But I would argue that our method gives a more realistic picture of the community's willingness for contact. Moreover, sub-dividing the community into four groups is not just a statistical exercise. It has helped to redefine the community in terms of their likely response to mentally handicapped people and reminded us that the needs of each group, in terms of preparation for contact, could be different. The challenge is to expand the size of the Ready group by reducing the numbers in the other three. Can we transform the Uncaring into the Willing, and the Unable into the Ready?

A starting point is to find out if the Readys have something which the others do not have. As you will read, we are right back where we started—confidence to meet mentally handicapped people.

THE CONFIDENT ARE READY

I'll forgive you if you feel we are beginning to go round in circles. Actually, it would be more accurate to describe it as a spiral. The people most ready to meet mentally handicapped peers are those with the highest average scores on the Confidence in Meeting Scale. By contrast, those with the lowest scores on this scale are on average in the Uncaring group, with people in the other two groups—Unable and Willing—in between. This correspondence held for four out of the five contact items—the exception was that of marriage which, as we noted earlier, had very few respondents who were prepared to encourage it.

Although the Confidence in Meeting measure was the most important way of distinguishing the four groups on all contact items, it was not the only one. But these varied according to the type of contact proposed. The uneven distribution of the groups on items one and five prevented full statistical analyses being undertaken. Hence, we shall focus on the people's readiness for the following contacts:

Sit beside you in bus/train or café

THE READYS	THE OTHERS
Women	Men
Over 40s	Under 30s
Regular contact with disabled people	No past contact
Above average score Confidence Scale	Below average score Confidence Scale

Join in social activities

THE READYS	THE OTHERS
Regular contact with disabled people	No past contact
Participate in three or more activities within the area	Participate in one or no activities
Know 15+ families in the area	Know three or fewer families
Above average score Confidence Scale	Below average score Confidence Scale

Wanted to be your friend

THE READYS	THE OTHERS
Regular contact with disabled people	No past contact
Resident in area of Day Centre	Resident in area of Group Home
Over 30s	Teens and twenties
Above average score Confidence Scale	Below average score Confidence Scale

As you can see, past contact with disabled people

features in all the lists. That, too, was a major factor in boosting people's Confidence in Meeting scores, but our statistical analysis takes that into account. These results therefore suggest that past contacts produce another effect, namely a readiness to contemplate social involvement with a disabled person.

On two out of the three items, age is also a factor—with younger people being *less* ready than their elders for contact with mentally handicapped people. This is certainly linked to their Confidence in Meeting scores but that cannot be the whole story, for their age would not have shown up in our analyses.

It might be that older people find one-to-one contacts (implied in items two and three) with mentally handicapped people easier because they approximate to the maternal/paternal rôle, whereas this rôle is denied to younger people and they have no ready alternative.

But the fact remains, younger people will require special attention if they are to become more ready to have contact with their mentally handicapped peers. The good news is that it can be done. Our book *Breaking Barriers* shows you how.

The other variables linked to readiness for contact are peculiar to specific contacts. Those linked with joining social activities are understandable—the more active you are socially, the more likely and ready you are to meet different people.

However, the link between a readiness to sit beside people and gender and greater willingness of people in the vicinity of the Day Centre to befriend a mentally handicapped person, I leave to your ingenuity to explain. Although, as we will see in Chapter 8, it was the people in this area who also expressed interest in a scheme for having a mentally handicapped person lodge with the family for short periods.

What, then, should be our strategy in preparing the community for contacts with mentally handicapped people? These results provide a number of pointers.

READINESS VARIES ACCORDING TO TYPE OF CONTACT PROPOSED

A number of implications then flow from that proposition:

1 There is no absolute number of people in the community who are ready and willing to have contact with mentally handicapped people. One cannot talk about it as being depressingly low or surprisingly high, unless one spells out the type of contact that is envisaged.

2 Some people will be comfortable with one form of contact and will possibly try to avoid other forms. Hence, in recruiting voluntary helpers, some cognisance must be paid to their interests and lifestyle.

3 Certain subgroups in the community are more ready than others. Targeting your educational programmes and recruiting drives at them should maximise the returns on your effort. For example, our results suggest that people who are already socially active are more likely to be willing to share some of their social life with a handicapped person.

4 In general young people seem less ready than others. Special efforts may be needed to help them.

PAST CONTACT AFFECTS CONFIDENCE WHICH AFFECTS READINESS

Or put another way, if you have had little or no contact with mentally handicapped people, you will not be confident in meeting them and so will be less ready to accept contact. We need to transform that vicious circle into a productive spiral—having more contacts that produce more confidence which in turn produces more readiness for contacts which, when they occur, increases confidence further and boosts readiness which . . . need I go on?

Such spirals cannot start unless there is some personal—and pleasant—contact between local people and their disabled peers. As we saw in Chapter 4, that has been absent for the majority of the people in our study. Nor is the fault wholly theirs. If more disabled people had been involved in community life, the public might be more ready for further contacts rather than be classed by us as Willing, Unable or Uncaring.

Brian Rix,[57] in trying to explain why the British public gives a staggering £29 million to animal charities—seven times more than the amount given to mental health work—drew this analogy:

> Dogs are a far more familiar sight in most British streets than mentally handicapped people. We can meet dogs every day walking in the park, travelling on public transport, and on their way to the local pet parlour for a shampoo and set. Meanwhile many people who are mentally handicapped are permitted to stroll no further than the hospital grounds. If they travel at all they go in groups and generally use hospital transport. And when they want a hair cut, they go to the hospital hairdresser. No wonder the public feels more charitable towards dogs: mentally handicapped people are out of sight and out of mind.

Enough said.

7 Who Is My Neighbour?

> I feel I'm not as bright as other people might be. But at the same time, I think we should be allowed to have the chances others have in their lives.
>
> *Dublin man living in a Group Home for mentally handicapped people*

A chance to have a home of your own. The goal of community care policies in many countries is to do exactly that for many mentally handicapped people. Instead of going off to live in an institution, the idea is to provide these people with a house within the community. As the Jay Committee[11] put it, 'the accommodation we provide should be, in terms of size, design and location, as much like the accommodation we ourselves would wish to live in.' (p. 47)

There is a snag, however. What if the neighbours object to having a Group Home in their area? We all know instances when it has happened. In the USA, for example, various surveys[45] estimated that about one third of community residences encountered opposition to their opening; most of it coming from neighbours but also from local officials and politicians and, in a small number of cases, from parents of retarded residents.

And in Britain, some of the objections neighbours gave to opposing a community home for a group of people with Down's Syndrome, were reported in the local paper as follows:

> . . . it is a fact that all grades of mongols have committed murder and acts of violence.
>
> The house and garden won't be secure enough.

> We have a young grand-daughter who comes to visit us . . . there must be a chance that there is a danger to children and young people in the vicinity.

As Brian Rix[57] commented, 'the people who make this kind of remark are not monsters. They are ordinary, respectable men and women who are kind to dumb animals, pay their rates and abide by the laws of the land. Many are well educated. But they are quite ignorant about mental handicap.' (p. 4)

On the principle that it is better to be forewarned, we wondered:

* what the reactions of Dubliners would be to having mentally handicapped people living beside them;
* what problems they would foresee arising;
* what type of person is most likely to object.

This would be useful information when it came to planning further group homes within communities like the ones we surveyed.

PREVIOUS SURVEYS

The results from previous surveys suggested that only a small majority of people would 'prefer not', 'be unwilling' or would 'object' to having mentally handicapped people as next-door neighbours. The phrasing of the question varied from country to country, but as the Figure below shows, the proportions remained remarkably similar.

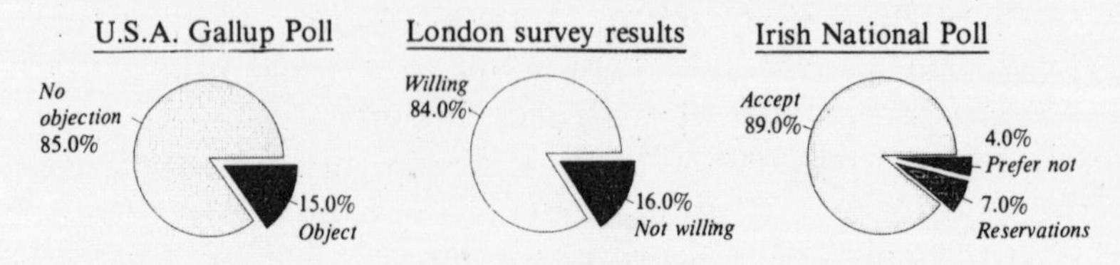

The USA Gallup Poll,[58] commissioned by the President's Committee on Mental Handicap, made mention of *six* mildly or moderately retarded persons 'occupying a home on your block' whereas the London survey[43] envisaged '*a* mentally handicapped person living next door.' In the Irish

National Poll,[41] the question referred to mentally handicapped people living in the neighbourhood.

It has been suggested that this is too rosy a picture. These people could claim to have no objections knowing that there was little likelihood of a home opening in their area. They might sing a different song if it were actually to happen.

A rather clever American study[36] put this notion to the test. If there was a house with a 'for sale' sign in the neighbourhood, they called on the people living immediately adjacent and, among other questions, dropped in the following: 'That house (indicating the direction of the target house with a gesture) is on the market. We would like to know what your views would be if that house was the location of a Group Home.'

Similar interviews were conducted with matched 'control' respondents where there was no 'threat' of a house opening. Lo and behold, there were small but statistically significant differences; twice as many people in the threat group had objections (20 per cent) compared to the control group (10 per cent). Still this meant that four out of five people had no objections.

Determining people's concerns

By contrast, the British poll for Mencap[42] used an entirely different technique. They presented all the people they interviewed with a listing of potential problems—14 in all—and asked them to say whether each one would be a concern to them if two mentally handicapped adults moved in next door. It appears that *everybody* chose at least one of the problems listed as being of concern to them. Quite a difference from the other polls!

But the Mencap list included concerns about the well-being of the handicapped people, for instance, 'They might not get enough professional care'; 'Local people/children might make fun of them'; 'They might feel isolated'. Indeed these were the three most commonly expressed concerns by upwards of two-thirds of people. Concerns about the effect on the neighbourhood or themselves, such as 'They might harm local children/people'; 'They might damage property' or 'Your home could lose value', were a major concern with one in five people at best—which is broadly in line with other polls.

However, this poll could also be accused of putting ideas into people's heads. If you present people with 14 possible problems it is highly likely that they will choose at least one. Or put another way, it would create a very bad impression to say they were not concerned 14 times! Moreover, no indication is given as to how the 14 possible problems were arrived at. The usual procedure is to carry out preliminary studies in which a comparable group is asked to list the problems they would foresee occurring. If this was done, then some rather esoteric items ended up on the list of problems, viz. 'They might harm pets'—a problem which I confess I had not heard expressed before. Yet amazingly, almost one in three people were concerned that this could happen; a higher proportion than those seeing a threat to their house value! Perhaps there is some truth in the British love of animals after all.

If the public do not know what to expect from 'strangers', then everything which they hold dear can appear to be threatened. All it needs is for one or two people to start speculating and, as the Mencap results suggest, rumours may spread.

A BETTER QUESTION?

How do you strike a balance between obtaining superficial replies—the criticism of the earlier polls—and the other extreme of exaggerating people's fears, which I suggest could have happened in the Mencap poll? Our solution was to take the best of both. We adapted the Mencap question as follows:

> 'If two mentally handicapped adults moved in next door to you, do you think that this would give rise to any problems in the neighbourhood?'

Three alternative answers were provided:

'No it wouldn't.
'Unsure'.
'Yes it would'.

If the third option was chosen, we went on to ask: 'Could you say what these might be?' and a probe, 'Anything else?', was also added.

This style of question would let us know the concerns which people expressed spontaneously, while at the same time giving an indication of the proportion of people who had no concerns. As you will see, the question seemed to work well.

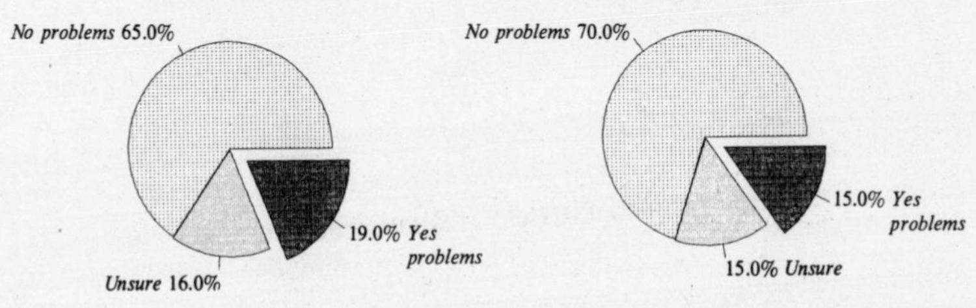

In both areas, the proportion of people giving each answer was similar. Those living in the area of the Day Centre might have been expected to raise more problems as they had no experience of a home. This was not the case.

Equally the existence of a Group Home in an area did not increase reports of problems. Similar results were found in the London neighbourhood study.[43] Before the hostel opened, 27 per cent of people were not willing to have a mentally handicapped person living next door to them, but three years later, with the hostel in full swing, the proportion of objectors had dropped to 16 per cent.

TWO-THIRDS FORESEE NO PROBLEMS

Unlike previous polls (see pp. 114–116), we found a much lower percentage of people reporting 'no problems'. It could be that the residents in these two areas were less disposed to having mentally handicapped people as neighbours, or indeed that the Irish are less hospitable, despite our national stereotype. Nationalities do differ in their expressed values and beliefs, as Gallup's International studies involving ten European countries clearly demonstrate.[59] But in order to make a valid comparison across nationalities or even within a country, precisely the same question has to be asked. A change of wording—no matter how slight—can produce a different interpretation.

But a preoccupation with percentages will blind us to the more important issue—listening to people's concerns. So let's forget about the quantity for a moment and look at the width of their concerns.

CONCERNS

In our study 73 people (17 per cent) mentioned one or more problems they could foresee arising. By far the most frequent—over half of all mentions—was that children or young people in the area would make fun of handicapped people, tease them or jeer at them. Indeed, the uppermost 'problem' in most people's minds—be they Irish or British—seemed to be the well-being of the mentally handicapped people. This is illustrated in the table opposite, where all the different concerns are listed in rank order, from the most frequently mentioned to the least mentioned.

It does not take much analysis to see the inherent contradictions in such a listing of concerns. Some people view the mentally handicapped as defenceless innocents, unable to protect themselves and easily taken advantage of. Others see them as a threat, especially to children or property, and express feelings of embarrassment at being in their company. Indeed, the same people will express both types of concern, never realising that they are being inconsistent or, some would say, irrational. When you are not quite sure what to expect, I guess it is reasonable to suppose that anything might happen.

Nevertheless, as the ranking showed, concern for the

Concerns expressed about having mentally handicapped people as neighbours.

Concerns	*Rank Order**	
	Ireland	*Britain*
FOR WELL-BEING OF HANDICAPPED PEOPLE		
Made fun of, teased, jeered at	1	1
Taken advantage of, victimised	2	–
Need somebody to help them, need professional care	5.5	2
Their property would be vandalised	11	–
They might keep to themselves	11	3
They would stand out from other people	11	–
People would not have time to look after them	13	5
FOR EFFECTS ON COMMUNITY LIFE		
People would be shy, embarrassed in their company	3.5	7
Danger to children, parents would keep kids away	3.5	4
People couldn't communicate with them	7.5	–
There would be complaints from other people	7.5	–
Property devalued	9	11
They could be violent, not responsible for actions	5.5	–
PROBLEMS INCLUDED IN BRITISH STUDY NOT MENTIONED BY IRISH PEOPLE		
They might cause noise/disturbance		6
They might damage property		8
You would miss the company of normal neighbours		9
They might harm pets		10
Children might become friendly with them		12
Friends might avoid visiting you		13
You would be afraid to leave your home		14

N.B. Twenty-four people in our study gave a vague response, most usually along the lines of 'it would depend on their level of disability', but they did not spell out what these might be.

* When two or more problems have the same frequency of mention, they are given an average of the ranks. For example, if the fourth and fifth ranked items tied, each item is ranked as 4.5.

handicapped people outstripped problems which the other members of the community might face. Indeed, traditional worries—such as a fall in property values—came low on the list.

Only seven per cent of people in our survey mentioned deleterious effects on community life; it was six per cent in the London neighbourhood[43] survey. But prior to the hostel opening, 26 per cent of the Londoners had mentioned disadvantages for the community.

Child Safety—One concern that should perhaps be taken more seriously is that of children's safety. It not only came top in our survey and the Mencap poll, but it was the most frequently mentioned concern of Londoners before the hostel opened; it is referred to in nearly all the American studies and a recent investigation in Israel[26] identified it as a distinct factor linked with active opposition to community residences.

The fear may be irrational and the risk even less than with non-handicapped neighbours, but it is a point worth exposing as a myth. For instance, fewer than one per cent of 1,804 developmentally disabled residents living in the community had been in police custody over a two-year period.[60] Out of 151 mentally handicapped adults living in foster family care in New York for, on average, 12 years, there were two instances of shop-lifting and no reports of interfering with children.[21]

Alternatively, some have argued that mentally handicapped people are better placed in communities with few young children.[61] It is a more normal setting for them, the likelihood of teasing by children is minimised and elder neighbours may have more time for them.

WHO'S WORRIED?

Finally, can we identify the people in the community who are most likely to foresee problems? In our study and to a lesser extent in the Mencap poll, one characteristic stands out—the people most likely to express concerns are those who have had past contact with mentally handicapped people and/or met the people from the local centre. That of course ties in with the type of concerns most frequently expressed, namely teasing, nobody to look after them, etc. But there were signs that these were the people who also had concerns about adverse effects on community life. Unfortunately the numbers were so small in our data that we could not explore this point as fully as we would have liked or as it deserves. If it were true, then gone is the idea that opposition to community facilities usually comes from scaremongers who know little or nothing about mental handicap. Here's how some of our people expressed their concerns:

I'm very sympathetic towards mentally handicapped people. I think they are unfortunate. I wouldn't mind living next door but I couldn't have one in my house. Man (40s).

Got to be very careful with the mentally handicapped. Watch them very carefully. Woman (50s).

Wouldn't bother me if mentally handicapped person lives next door—or physically handicapped. Bit of a hassle for them to live. I'd like to see people like this living in this estate and getting along with people. Man (20s).

Won't have any objections to mentally handicapped (living next door). Often would be more wary of normal people. Man (40s).

RISKS NOT PROBLEMS

With hindsight I wonder if we have not confused the public and ourselves by talking about 'problems' and 'concerns' when what we mean are 'risks'. It is futile to debate whether the 'problem' is real or imaginary. Rather we need to establish the likelihood or risk of that event occurring, such as the mentally handicapped people not getting enough professional care, or of them causing damage to people's property or of property values falling.

Of course some people play safe and are not prepared to accept any risk. They imagine what could go wrong and do not want to chance it. Phrased in these terms, it is quite likely that some parents and relatives of handicapped people and even professional workers will feature among the 'no risk-takers' as well as members of the public. Indeed I know many parents of older handicapped adults who would be appalled at the prospect of their son or daughter living unsupervised in a strange neighbourhood, even though the professional staff know that he or she is well able to do so.

Protagonists for community services need to make three sorts of risk-assessments. First, how likely it is that mentally handicapped people in general, or more especially the ones they nominate for community living, will exhibit the undesirable behaviours listed in the Table earlier. I am sure they are well used to doing this, but I wonder how much they publicise their conclusions and the evidence on which they are based.

Secondly, how will they minimise the risk of mentally handicapped people being left without support and backup, or becoming isolated in their house? What assurances can be given to concerned neighbours?

Thirdly, we need to know what the public—and especially prospective neighbours—are prepared to risk. This is a less practised skill but it might be tackled as follows. I would adapt the question used by ourselves and in the Mencap poll in the following way:

> 'If two mentally handicapped adults moved in next door to you, do you think this would give rise to any risks either for them or for other people in the neighbourhood? First, would there be risks for them?'

Three alternative answers could be provided:

None that I can think of.

Unsure.

Yes, there would.

People choosing the last option could then be shown a listing of possible 'risks' taken from the Table, and asked to rate whether each would have a 'high risk', 'some risk' or 'little risk' of occurring in their area. Finally, they could be asked if they had any other risks in mind.

In the second part of the question, people would be asked:

'Would there be any risks for the other people in the neighbourhood?' The three answers used in part one would be repeated here, as would a second listing of possible risks for those choosing 'Yes' (e.g. taken from the Table). The more astute among you will have spotted that we have avoided putting ideas of risks into the heads of those who think there are none, but we do 'force' them to think about handicapped people's needs separately from effects on the neighbourhood.

Some further refinements might include:

a) a brief description of the characteristics of the mentally handicapped people you have in mind, e.g. trained to look after themselves;
b) The inclusion in the listings of potential risks expressed previously by people in that area or by parents/professionals in the service;
c) using the same questions in contrasting neighbourhoods, e.g. those with young families and those without.

MINIMISING COMMUNITY OPPOSITION

For some,[62] the solution to minimising opposition has been to adopt a 'Machiavellian' approach—open the home with the minimum of fuss and advance notice, so that potential opponents do not have the opportunity to co-ordinate a

protest. And anyway, most available research[45] suggests that once the home opens, community opposition decreases. In fact some of the most vocal opponents can end up becoming the strongest supporters.

Others argue,[63] rightly so in my opinion, that the result may be ultimately counter-productive in that the neighbours are at best indifferent and uninvolved with the home. They may perceive it as a development which was foisted upon them and for which they have no responsibility. The house and the people in it 'belong' to the service agency, not to that community.

The alternative strategy is to build up trust and support from within the community through exchanging information and gaining their co-operation. Among the techniques which have proved successful are:

* Send a letter to all residents in the vicinity and then visit door-to-door to answer questions.
* Give the neighbours the opportunity to visit similar residences and meet mentally handicapped people.
* Use local contacts—friends, known supporters—to spread the word and feed back reactions. For example, you can have mentally handicapped people at small gatherings in their homes prior to opening a home nearby.
* Recruit staff for the home from the locality.
* Place some mentally handicapped people from that locality in the group home. Or have the prospective residents already engaged in some pursuits within that district, e.g. using the leisure facilities or doing voluntary work, before they come to live in the area.
* People from the community might visit their prospective neighbours prior to them moving in. When this was done in the USA[64] the people who visited were able to convince the opponents in their district that their fears were ungrounded.
* Organise presentations and workshops for civic,

community and church leaders, with mentally handicapped people as speakers or panelists. Voluntary organisations should consult and liaise with local councillors and 'town hall' officials.

* Appoint some people from the area to your Planning Board or team which is making arrangements for housing of residents.
* Counteract misinformation about dangers or fall in property values, e.g. No incidents of harm have occurred in neighbourhoods where Group Homes are already established. Neighbours from another area might 'testify' to this, e.g. on video.

  There is no evidence from community studies of a loss in property values.[65] The homes in the community are well-kept. Illustrate with map and slide shows.
* Give assurances about supervision—who's available and how they can be contacted.
* Arrange for local newspaper articles and/or features on local radio about mentally handicapped people, emphasising their abilities, feelings, ambitions, etc.
* Involve mentally handicapped people in community planning meetings and in testifying at public hearings.
* Maintain neighbours' interest when the home gets going by having 'open house' days, suppers, etc. Encourage 'volunteer' involvement but in a planned and structured way (see Chapter 9). Have community representatives on Planning Boards for existing and new developments.

The essential prerequisite to all these strategies can be easily summarised.

YOU MUST KNOW THE COMMUNITY AS WELL AS YOU KNOW THE MENTALLY HANDICAPPED PEOPLE MOVING INTO GROUP HOMES

The careful assessment which goes into selecting people

for community residences must be complemented by equally detailed information about the community, e.g. the type of people living there; their past responses to similar situations and their present concerns; the social networks which exist and who are the acknowledged community leaders.

Armed with this information you may decide that a Machiavellian approach is the most appropriate, for instance in communities where there is high turn-over and diversity, such as 'flat-land'. Conversely, a collaborative strategy with residents and community leaders is a must when dealing with settled, owner-occupier communities.

In communities where there is little cohesiveness it might be sufficient to deal with community leaders, such as the parish priest or local elected representatives.

You cannot decide until you have reliable information about the community, from first-hand experience, contacts with representatives or by undertaking a local survey (see Chapter 10).

Richard Hogan's[63] conclusions are worth bearing in mind:

> Dealing directly with the concerns of the local community may be more difficult than simply establishing the home as a 'fait accompli', but attempts to avoid opposition can backfire with disastrous effects . . . The most normal and least restrictive setting is not a monastery or a utopian community without conflict. Residential communities are rife with petty squabbles and occasionally hostile confrontations. Seeking to avoid these marks a retreat from the community. (p. 125)

The fundamental question remains: do we really want our Group Homes to be part of the community, or merely located in it? There is a difference.

8 Who Wants To Know?

> I was in outside employment for a while. I didn't really like it. I felt some people did not know what I was . . . If they knew I was mildly, they would not have touched me at all. In my last job, people realised it and thought I was a human being like they were, and they weren't doing anything stupid and ridiculous.
>
> *Unemployed man living in a Group Home*

There's an old English proverb which goes something like this:

> He who knows not and knows not that he knows not, is a fool—avoid him. He who knows not and knows that he knows not, is a wise man—teach him.

Perhaps it is rather much to describe our community as made up of fools and wise men, but this proverb summarises well the substance of our experience. In this chapter we shall be providing answers to questions such as:

* What do people want to know about mental handicap?
* What are their preferred ways of obtaining this information?
* Who are the people in the community who are most interested in finding out about mental handicap?
* How do they react to becoming involved in a scheme where mentally handicapped people lodge with families for short periods?

But before we get caught up in the results, I want to underscore the importance of listening to the public's preferences. Remember, we are dealing with people who have had relatively little experience of mental handicap;

there is much which we feel they ought to know if they are to cope successfully with the diverse effects of this disability. But too much information, too soon, will only confuse and demoralise the learners. It underscores their ignorance and inability to cope. The result—they stop listening. Why should they feel bad about themselves?

An alternative approach, much used now in health education, is to tailor your message to your listener's concerns. For instance, anti-smoking campaigns aimed at young people now stress the unpleasant smells which linger around smokers' clothes or on their breath. 'Who wants to kiss an ashtray?' was one effective punchline. This change in emphasis was because young people in the prime of their health could not conceive of themselves as dying from lung cancer thirty years on. A distant death was of little concern compared to their present preoccupation with appearances. The old adage of successful salespeople —give the customer what they want, when they want it—was rediscovered anew.

Bear that in mind as you read about what our people were prepared to learn about mental handicap.

WHAT DO PEOPLE WANT TO KNOW ABOUT MENTAL HANDICAP?

What do I do if I meet a mentally handicapped person?

What causes it?

Those are the two most popular topics whenever we ask people what information they would like to have on mental handicap. We decided *not* to include it in the door-to-door survey, principally because we had asked this question of so many people (more than 1,700) in other studies, and always the same answers came up. For example, the Figure below shows the results obtained for a group of more than 400 evening class attenders and sales staff in city centre stores—referred to as 'Neighbours'—and for a group of 120 staff and voluntary helpers in services for handicapped people. These we call, 'Friends'.

The topics were listed on a questionnaire and for each one the person could select one of three answers: *'Very much'* (like to have this information); *'Maybe'* (like to have

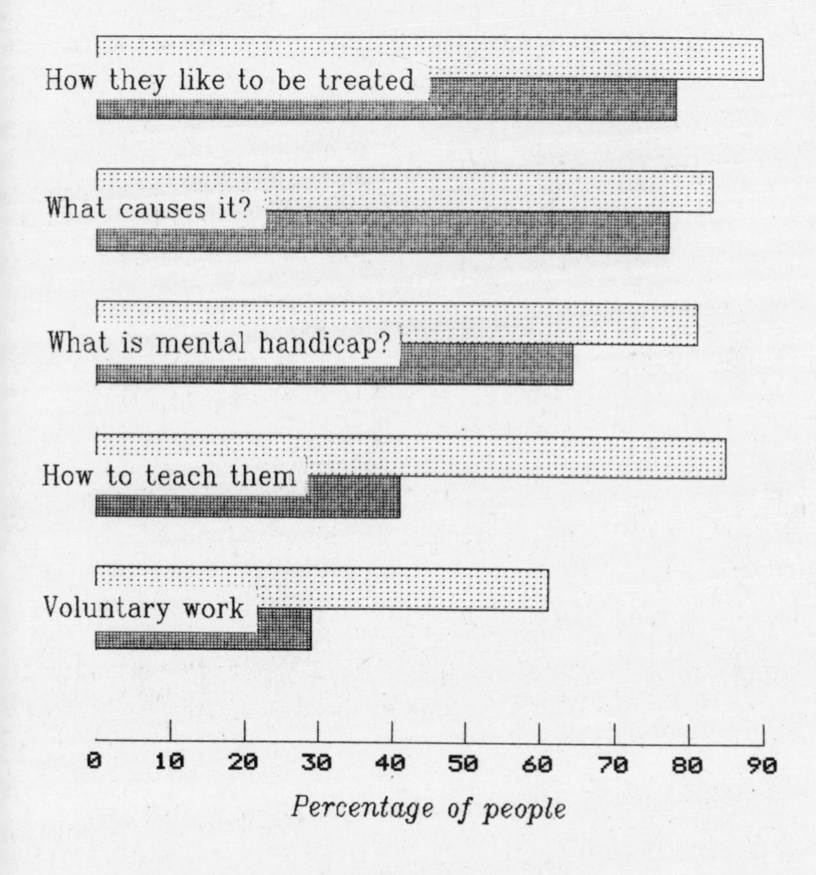

this information); *'No'* (would not want to have this information). The middle option was included for those people who find it difficult to say *No*, as well as for those who genuinely cannot make up their minds. However, only people saying *Yes* are included in the final results.

The significant finding in a Figure such as this is not the precise percentage against each item—that can vary from one sample to the next. Rather it is the *pattern* of results across the items and groups because that is likely to be more stable. Two themes can be identified in the Figure:

1 *Friends* show more interest in all the topics, a predictable finding but one which helps to confirm the validity of the question.
2 The more popular topics are those which personally affect the individual, such as, how do you best interact with them (Item 1 and also Item 4 in the case of *Friends*) and, could it ever happen to me (one interpretation of their interest in the causes of mental handicap—Item 2)? By contrast, those items which involve meeting a disabled person (Items 4 and 5) are chosen least often by the *Neighbours*.

Preparing to meet

Everyone's dominant concern—including those who are familiar with disabled people—is to know more about how best to get along with them. This need is not easily met. First, as we saw in Chapter 2, there is the tremendous diversity of people who are called mentally handicapped. Just because a person can cope with one individual is not a guarantee of confidence in coping with others.

Secondly, handicapped people by definition are often not able and/or not encouraged to convey their likes and dislikes. One cannot be sure what they are getting out of interactions with other people, as sometimes they give very little feedback.

Thirdly, there are still disputes both among parents and among professionals as to what is best for disabled people.

Some say they only need love and care in the security of familiar surroundings, whereas others maintain that they need to get out and about, doing as much as they can for themselves, even if it means taking risks.

Hence, trite advice to the public on the lines of, 'treat them as you would anyone else', may be useless and could even be an anxiety intensifier.

One possibility is to give people succinct guidelines, on the theme of 'what to do if'. This might be done informally on a person-to-person level, or through watching videos or by reading a short pamphlet.

Another approach is for them to first meet mentally handicapped people in the company of a non-disabled person, such as a member of staff or better still a neighbour or friend of theirs, who knows the handicapped person and who can act as an intermediary. Once more handicapped people are integrated into normal patterns of social life, this form of education will occur more often.

There is a sense, too, in which information on how mentally handicapped people like to be treated has to be on-going. Remember this item also came top for the Friends. Opportunities for people to learn from each other by discussing their experiences and reactions seem the most feasible way of this coming about. Such reviews are an essential part of successful community schemes involving voluntary helpers.

Information on the causes of mental handicap

By contrast, this topic is more easily tackled. It can be done from a number of different angles. It could be linked to the individuals whom people already know, using them to illustrate the variety of conditions which can give rise to a disability. Alternatively, the emphasis could be on preventing disabling conditions with the message slanted towards actions which prospective parents might take to safeguard the well-being of their offspring. The choice of method, once again, will be determined by the needs of the audience you are addressing. A common mistake is merely to simplify the medical textbook instead of reworking the information to meet the needs of the consumers.

Finally, it goes without saying that knowing more about the causes of disability, or even about handicaps in general, does not ensure that the person is any better at getting on with disabled people. Surprisingly this truism tends to be forgotten in the training of professional workers, just as often as in community education.

HOW DO PEOPLE PREFER TO OBTAIN INFORMATION ABOUT MENTAL HANDICAP?

Finding out what people want to know is only half the story. We also need some indication of their preferred methods of acquiring information. Hence we presented the people in our study with six or seven alternatives (see Figure below) and asked them to select one of three answers: 'No', 'Maybe' or 'Yes'.

The sequence went like this: 'Would you watch a programme on TV about them? . . . (Answer) . . . read a leaflet about them? . . . (Answer) and so on. The percentages of people replying Yes and Maybe are shown in the Figure. Obviously there are other possibilities for learning more about mental handicap in addition to these, but our selection was intended to represent the different 'styles' which could be used rather than to provide an exhaustive menu.

The end result is a question or, more accurately, a series of related questions, which gives us two kinds of results.

First, we obtain a sensitive measure of people's willingness for information. To get this, we count the number of items to which they say 'Yes'. The highest score is therefore six (seven in the Group Home area), and the lowest is zero. By contrast, a single question such as, 'Would you be interested in finding out more about mental handicap?' would only yield a zero to one measure arising from the Yes/No answer. We shall discuss these findings under the heading, 'How interested are they in learning more?'

Secondly, we can gauge people's preferences for the different types of approach which could be used to present information to them; determining, for example, the people who are most likely to attend a meeting. We shall go into these results in some detail shortly.

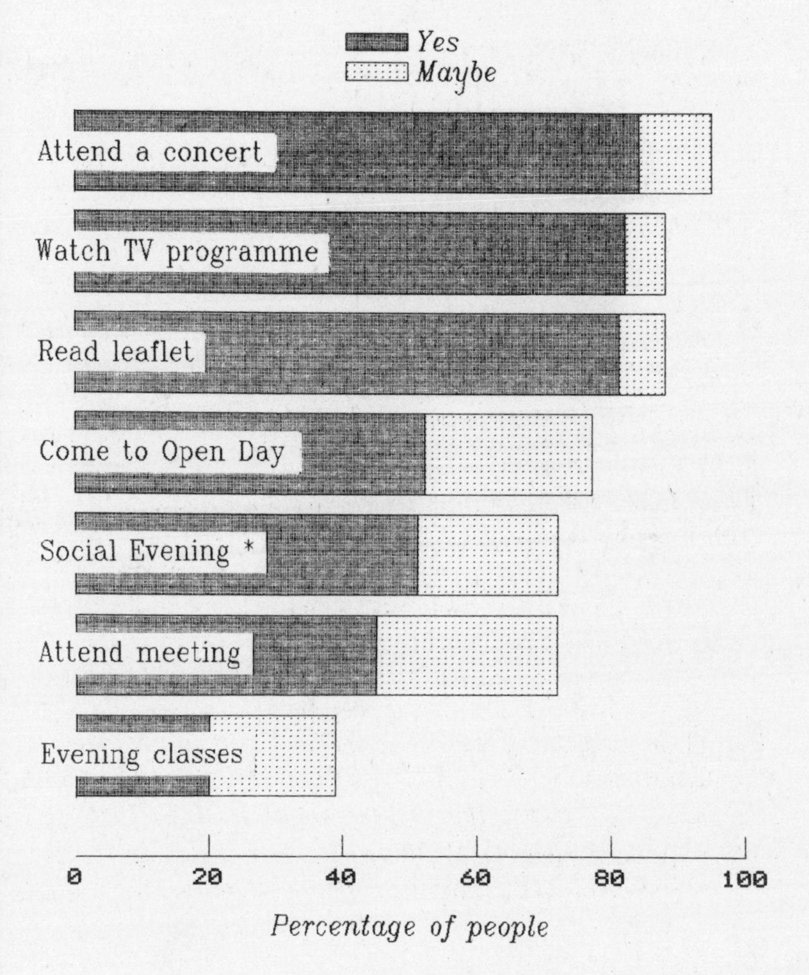

HOW INTERESTED ARE THEY IN LEARNING MORE?

Nearly everyone says they want to know more

People do seem interested in learning more. Almost 98 per cent of our people said 'Yes' to one or more items on the list, which means that only two per cent were totally uninterested (i.e. said 'No' or 'Maybe' to all the alternatives). That is a most encouraging finding, although some might say that it is over-optimistic. Perhaps a more realistic indicator of a person's interest is when they say 'Yes' not to just one item, but to at least four. That criterion does make a difference, but even then, more than half our people (54 per cent, to be precise) said 'Yes' to four or more of the items. In general, then, people are willing to know more about mental handicap, although, as we shall see, some are more interested than others.

Those most interested in knowing more

Three distinct, but overlapping features identify the interested person:

First, they have had personal contact with disabled people.
If they report meeting disabled people in general, or mentally handicapped people in particular, then on average they select more than five items from the list of alternatives. Likewise, those people who report two or more contacts with people from the local service top the poll with an average of five and a half items selected. It would appear that knowing some disabled people living in your locality is an incentive to learn more about them.

Second, they are well disposed to meeting mentally handicapped people.
Interested people not only have significantly higher scores on the Confidence Scale, but they also report a greater willingness to have contact with handicapped people, and they are more likely to feel that they will come into contact with them (see Chapter 6).

Third, their personal characteristics also play a part.
For example, women are more interested than men. That is a fairly predictable finding by now, but perhaps this next finding is more novel. Those people who report more social contacts within their area—for instance the number of families they know in the neighbourhood or the number of recreational activities they are involved in—are also the people who are more likely to be interested in learning more about mental handicap. In short, the more active a rôle you play within the community, the more disposed you are to widen your horizons.

For clarity, we have described these three features as though they were quite separate. In reality they are interlinked. For instance, we know that women are more disposed than men to meeting disabled people. Hence the final step is to ask which one of three features is the most likely to distinguish interested people. The computer analysis gave a clear answer:

> *Those most interested in knowing more are the people who are well disposed to meeting handicapped people*

Implications
These findings are the opposite of a commonly held belief, namely that you must first inform people about mental handicap before you can risk letting them meet disabled people. Instead our recommendation turns that belief around. *Once the public are comfortable with the prospect of meeting mentally handicapped people, they will be more interested in learning about the disability.*

Practice must precede the theory. A bus driver we interviewed had this to say:

> *My experience is with a mentally handicapped boy who travels on the buses. He would be lost only for the buses. We take him for a drive and he talks to us, makes conversation and has a laugh. Travelling on the buses is good for them. They get out.*

WHO'S PREPARED TO DO WHAT?

Now let's look in more detail at the particular ways people might get information. But first a warning. I've said it before but it is well worth repeating: the danger with questions of this type is that we have no guarantee that people would actually do what they say they would be prepared to do. Hence it is not the actual percentages against each item that are significant but rather the *pattern* which emerges as you read down the listing of options shown in the Figure on p. 133.

As you have no doubt spotted, the first three items were clear favourites and it is not hard to see what they have in common. They require no personal contact with disabled people; no special effort or commitment is needed and they can be done on the person's terms and in their own time. Unfortunately none of these seem to allow for the one essential ingredient in successful education—personal contact with a disabled peer.

Or maybe we need to challenge that presumption. Would it not be possible to marry the medium—concerts, TV or leaflets—to the messages you want to convey? For example, at a concert, the programme sellers and ushers could be disabled people and some of those with artistic talents might even participate in the show. Television can give viewers an opportunity of seeing and hearing disabled people, be it through soap operas (as was done in the popular British serial *Crossroads*), current affairs, plays and documentaries. Likewise, magazines and newspaper articles, even a leaflet if well illustrated with photographs, can convey something about their personalities. None of these will be ideal for the ultimate goals we may have in mind—the recruitment of volunteer helpers, say—but that is no excuse for ignoring the possibilities of the media or, worse still, using them ineptly. Their capacity to reach large numbers of people at little *per capita* cost cannot be equalled.

Even so, certain problems remain unresolved, for example:

Don't know much about it (mental handicap). If I see it on TV I get upset. Woman (30s).

Who are you working for—the Government or a charitable organisation? Will I be getting leaflets about these things sent to me? Woman (30s).

Attending meetings

The Irish do have the reputation for being gregarious, I know, but we were rather surprised by the sizeable proportion of people who seem prepared to attend an open day, social evening or meeting in *their* area. Note the emphasis. Now if these dispositions could be turned into bottoms on seats or feet in the door, then there could be a good chance of encouraging at least a proportion of attenders to become more involved with disabled people.

A useful starting point is to have some idea as to the type of person who is most likely to attend. Once again the computer readily supplied the answer. In a nutshell—*women who have had some contact with people from the local Centre and who score high on the Confidence in Meeting scale*. More details now follow for each type of event. Although they appeal to much the same group there are some significant discrepancies.

Open days and social evenings—Of the women, 62 per cent say they would attend compared to 39 per cent of men, as would 69 per cent of those who have had some contact with people from the local Centre, compared to 45 per cent of those reporting no contact. But in the case of a social evening at the Group Home, 86 per cent of those who say they would attend will have had some previous contact with the residents. Attendances are likely to be higher, too, from those people who are in regular contact with disabled people—68 per cent compared to 40 per cent of those with little or no previous contacts. Not surprisingly, the mean scores on the Confidence in Meeting scale are higher by one and a half points on average (15.7 versus 14.1) for people willing to attend open days and by more than two points (16.1 versus 13.9) for those thinking of coming to social evenings.

Meetings to learn more—Much the same pattern of results held for this option—likely attenders would be women who had met disabled people from the local Centre or who were in contact with disabled people in general—but there was also a significant additional characteristic. People who were already involved in two or more activities within their local community, were more likely to come to a meeting (56 per cent) than were those people who had no local involvement (34 per cent). Thus a person's contacts generally with people in the locality, as well as with disabled people, seem to prompt a greater willingness for further community involvement.

Evening classes—This option had only minority support (20 per cent) and that precluded the detailed statistical analysis which we were able to carry out with previous items.

However, the indications were that this option, too, attracted people fitting the descriptions given above.

Incidentally, it is highly unlikely that all 20 per cent of these people would ever turn up for evening classes. We might have obtained a more accurate estimate by asking an additional question, namely, 'Have you attended evening classes during the past year?' or, 'Have you *ever* attended evening classes?' The percentage of previous attenders who say they would also attend classes on mental handicap would probably give a more realistic estimate of the actual percentage of the public likely to attend evening classes.

But, I repeat, our main concern was not with overall percentages but rather to determine who in the community was disposed to know more about mental handicap. I think we have succeeded in doing that. We leave the last words to some of our interviewees:

> *Handicapped should be integrated into community; barriers should be broken down but the time the general public have to get involved is limited.* Male (30s).

> *Answers not necessarily because of mentally handicapped but wouldn't attend things anyway.* Male (30s).

> *Voluntary work with old people or the mentally handicapped. I'm thinking about it but don't know how to go about it.* Male (30s).

Our final question in this section was designed to test people's reactions in a more precise way: how they would feel about getting involved in helping to care for a mentally handicapped person.

WHO'S INTERESTED IN SHARING THEIR HOME WITH A MENTALLY HANDICAPPED PERSON?

This is the question we asked:

> *There's talk of a scheme in which people are paid to have a mentally handicapped person stay at their house for a weekend. Would you . . . ?*

The question was followed by four alternatives, one of which they were asked to select:

* be interested in having a person stay with you
* be interested but would want to know more about the scheme first
* be interested but it is not possible at present
* Not interested

Of course there are other ways by which ordinary people could become involved in helping. It certainly would have been interesting to know how they would have reacted to various propositions, but in the end—and by now we were getting to the end of what had been a long interview by door-step standards—we decided to opt for only the one scheme. Our reasoning was as follows. Domiciliary care schemes of this sort are by now well established for children and adults alike,[25] so the question was not fanciful. They can be succinctly described and payments were mentioned, not just because they invariably feature in such schemes but also to highlight that this was a different idea from traditional voluntary work.

Interested but . . .

Once again we cannot be sure that people would actually take a person into their homes, and we certainly have no information as to their motives for so doing. Nevertheless,

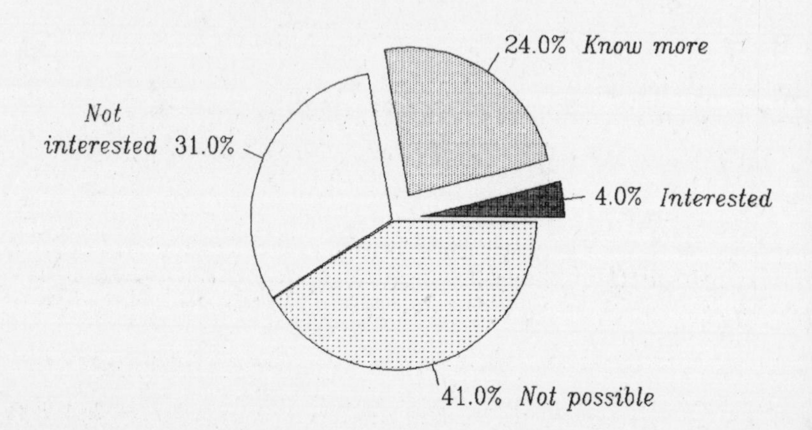

we have some indication that a proportion of people in the community are willing to consider the possibility.

Unfortunately the four per cent declaring interest without any reservations number only 15 people in our sample, which precludes statistical analyses. Instead we combined them with the group who expressed themselves interested but first wanted more information. The features that distinguished these people from the remainder were: higher scores on the Confidence in Meeting scale; more regular contact in the past with both disabled and mentally handicapped people; and knowing more families in the neighbourhood—all of which seems very plausible. This time women were no more interested than men and contact with people from the local Centre had no significant effect.

Here are some first-hand comments:

If I had a house I'd be willing to take them. Woman (20s).

Welcome to contact us if you want to send one for a weekend. Male (50s).

I'd be afraid I'd get emotionally involved. Male (40s).

Great things they're doing nowadays for disabled people. Male (40s).

Thus there is a sizeable group of people in the community who appear willing to contemplate this possibility, largely because they have had regular contact with disabled people and are reasonably confident of their ability to cope.

And even if our figure of four per cent saying they are interested straight off was an over-estimate by ten times, it still suggests that, in a community of 10,000 adults, there would be 40 people willing to look after a handicapped person for at least a day or two at a time. Why do the pessimists think that nobody in the community cares but themselves?

CONCLUSIONS

People are interested in knowing more about mental

handicap. There was little evidence that attitudes such as, 'What's it got to do with me?' or, 'It would upset me to think about them' are commonly held. If so, our people managed to disguise them pretty well.

On the other hand, it would be an exaggeration to depict the populace as eager students. But some people, particularly those who have been in contact with disabled people, are well disposed to learning more. To summarise, then:

* People's interest in mental handicap can be stimulated by giving them the opportunity to meet disabled people, particularly those in their own neighbourhood.
* Their need for guidance on how best to act with disabled people must be met so that their self-confidence is boosted.
* People's interest in the causes of mental handicap should be tuned to their interests and needs.
* Our messages about disability may have to be married to the media which people prefer, even though they are not ideal from our point of view.
* We must recognise the different levels of interest which exist within the community and adapt our messages accordingly. Our ambition for people who are 'apathetic' is that they will become 'interested'; that those who are now 'interested' might be transformed into 'activists'; and that present 'activists' are encouraged to be 'executives'—initiating their own schemes. But each transformation will need to be handled in a different way, so we cannot think in terms of one community education programme for everyone. Rather, you need to identify the priority target groups in your community and plan to meet their needs (see Chapter 10).

That said, I am only too conscious that ambitions and intentions about community education far outstretch the motivation and resources to make it happen. Families demand it, professionals prescribe it and Government reports applaud it, but who's going to do it? Ay, there's the rub!

9 Who Will Lend a Hand?

I do half it; then I have a brother and he knows, he's quicker; he'd have it done by the time you'd start yourself.

Trainee in workshop

Fund-raising is the traditional way for the public to help disabled people. By all accounts, they are willing to give generously. For example, in the Irish National Poll,[41] 66 per cent of people interviewed were agreeable to paying extra taxes to help people with disabilities. In fact they came out well ahead of old people, unemployed youth, children and itinerants. Likewise a Gallup poll[49] in Britain reported 58 per cent in agreement that 'local services for the sick and disabled should be extended even if it means some increase in rates.'

Several of the people we interviewed were involved in fund-raising:

I'd do all I could to help the handicapped money-wise like, I always do when they come round. Woman (50s).

I did the pools for spastic children for a few years and gave it up when I found that one penny in every six pennies went to the children, the rest went on administration. Woman (30s).

Good idea to do something for the handicapped—even a regular person to collect money to give to the mentally handicapped. Woman (40s).

My favourite story about fund-raising is that told by Liz Thompson[66] in her highly readable book about bringing up her Down's Syndrome son, James. She was a stall holder at a sale-of-work organised by the local Mencap group, and James, who was ten at the time, was helping. Towards the end of the day, he nonchalantly took ten pence out of the cash-box and set off to spend it. When challenged, he retorted, 'It's for the mentally handicapped, isn't it?'

Raising money is both an art and a science. It has gone on for centuries and no doubt will continue to do so, but latterly there has been a greater appreciation of a peculiar dilemma facing fund-raisers. Brian Rix[57] put it well:

> On the one hand we must present a positive image of mentally handicapped people, to persuade the public to accept them as friends and neighbours. On the other, we must encourage the view that extra resources in the form of state funds and voluntary donations, should be made available to meet their special needs.

One solution, as he rightly suggests, 'lies in showing both sides of the coin . . . the multiply handicapped toddler as well as the teenage athlete who ran in the London marathon.' Another is to draw a parallel with donations made for non-handicapped people, such as raising money to enable athletes to take part in Special Olympics.

It will take some artistry to break down the aura of sympathy, sadness and helplessness which pervades the public's view of disability while at the same time maintaining or increasing the amount of money donated.

FRIEND-RAISING NOT FUND-RAISING IS THE PRIORITY

Arguably the greater challenge though, is to encourage the public to give of their time and talents rather than their money. 'Friend-raising' (Sue Vineyard's catch-phrase) is an unexplored area, especially in the context of mental handicap. Yet if care by the community is to mean anything, ordinary men and women will have to give up some of their 'free' time to help people who are mentally handicapped. But are they prepared to lend a hand?

We decided to get answers to the following questions:

* What type of 'voluntary work' most appeals to people?
* Under what conditions are people prepared to offer their services? In particular, what incentive might we use to attract and maintain their interest?
* Who are the people most interested in helping?

The answers, to our surprise, confirmed Susan Ellis's[67] admonition—stop being amazed that people are prepared to volunteer!

First, though, a word of explanation about the survey. It was carried out separately from the door-to-door interviews we have been focusing on up to now. If the truth be told, it had not occurred to us to include this topic when we were drafting the questionnaire. But, as the results came in, it became very apparent that we needed the answers if we were to round off the story. We opted to take a quota sample, stratified by age and sex, of 100 people in each area. To speed things up we positioned ourselves in the local shopping centres and approached people as they came and went, checking first that they were from the neighbourhood. A copy of the questionnaire is given in the Appendix.

This procedure worked well for us—the shopping centre sample not only matched the previous door-to-door sample on age and sex as it was designed to do, but the two samples were also comparable in terms of previous contact with mentally handicapped people and knowledge of the local services (see Chapter 4).

EXPERIENCE OF VOLUNTARY WORK

We began by enquiring about the voluntary work people had done either in the past or were currently engaged in.

One in four had done voluntary work

Although only eight of the 200 people interviewed were presently engaged in voluntary work, over one quarter had some experience. A wide range of activities was cited, including helping the elderly, children, teenagers and handicapped people, through youth organisations (e.g. Scouts), churches (e.g. Legion of Mary) or community groups such as Civil Defence and St Vincent de Paul.

The bulk of the volunteers were in the 20-to-39-year group. Other than this, there were no features distinguishing those who had done voluntary work and those who had not. For example, women were no more likely than men.

There were 14 'volunteers' who had come into contact with mentally handicapped people. Interestingly, most of these were under 20 years old and, with one exception, none were over 40. It is possible that we had something to do with this. In recent years secondary schools throughout Ireland have begun to use the CARA programme with their senior pupils. This six-session module, produced by St Michael's and the Health Education Bureau, introduces teenagers to mental handicap and gives them the opportunity to meet disabled peers from a neighbouring Centre (see *Breaking Barriers*[1] for further details). We have since discovered that two of the three schools in the areas where the interviews took place had used the programme.

But how willing are people to do voluntary work in the future? That's the 64,000-dollar question. We waited until near the end of the interview to ask it.

Having described various ways in which volunteers could help (see p. 148), we asked, 'If some of these schemes were available in your area, would you be interested in getting involved?' Three alternative answers were provided, plus a supplementary question in which we enquired whether they would like further details posted to them. If they answered Yes, they gave their name and address. Thus the replies could be grouped into four categories:

* Not possible at present
* Perhaps
* Yes—no details requested
* Yes—requested further details.

As the Figure shows, one in ten people were sufficiently

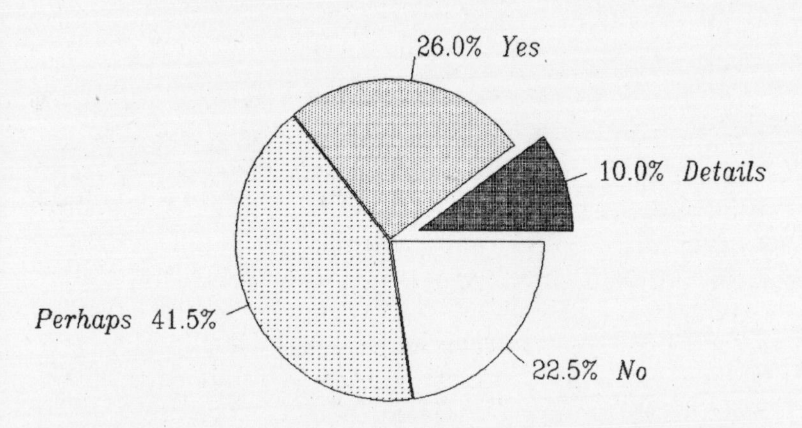

interested to request further details. It is unlikely that all of this group would want to become involved, but even if only one tenth of them did, it would mean that in a neighbourhood of about 3,000 people you would have potentially 30 volunteers. Conversely, if you could interest half or more, you would have more than 150 people to call upon. And that's discounting all the people who said 'yes' and 'perhaps'.

Significantly, the people most interested in having more details were the very ones who already had experience of mental handicap through voluntary work. Over one third of this group (36 per cent) requested details, compared with five per cent who had never undertaken voluntary work. Even those people who had done voluntary work in the past but who had no contact with people who were mentally handicapped were not particularly interested—only eight per cent of them requested further details. It would appear once again, that it is prior contact with mentally handicapped people which wins the public over.

Here are some reactions from the shoppers we spoke to:

Voluntary work is only for young people. Woman (50s).

We pay enough tax to the Government. People shouldn't be asked to work on a voluntary basis. Man (40s).

Government can only do so much; ordinary people have to get involved. Woman (20s).

People don't seem to be interested in voluntary work lately. Woman (40s).

TYPE OF HELP

There are many different ways in which ordinary men and women could be of help. Rather than bombard an unsuspecting public with an apparently endless listing, we chose six different themes and provided examples of what they would mean in practice. We began, 'There are different ways of helping mentally handicapped people. These are some of them (showing list on form). In the future, if you had the spare time . . .' Then followed six questions, to which the person replied, 'Yes'; 'Maybe'; 'Prefer not'.

1 *Would you go to their house?* e.g. to babysit, help with housework, help someone with their reading.
2 *Could they come to your house for a visit?* e.g. to give their family a break.
3 *Could they join you in something you already do?* e.g. shopping, sport, hobby, walks.
4 *Would you go along with a mentally handicapped person to night classes, cinema, etc?*
5 *Would you become a helper with a group/club for mentally handicapped people?*
6 *Would you lend a hand at special events?* e.g. sports days, sales of work, transport them, etc.

We decided to ask this question of everyone, and not just those people who were interested in doing voluntary work. We needed some clues to what appealed to people in general and not just to the 'converted'. When we checked to see if there was a difference between these two groups, the pattern of results was much the same, although people interested in doing voluntary work had a higher percentage of 'Yes' answers throughout (around 25 per cent more).

As you can see from the Figure, a majority of people

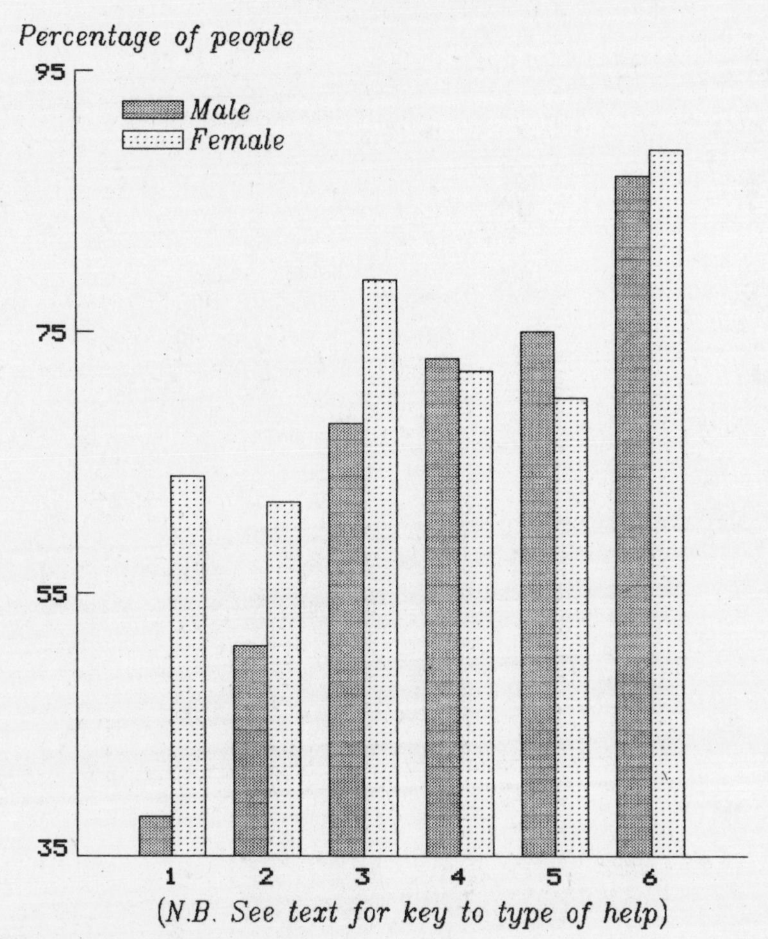

(N.B. See text for key to type of help)

expressed an interest in all six ways of helping. Of course, it is easy for people to say they will help if there is not much chance of it happening, so do not make the mistake of using the actual percentages as a guide. They are probably a gross over-estimate, although they could indicate a latent altruism which is there to be tapped.

Rather, our interest was in the differences between people's responses to the items and hence the pattern which emerges, i.e. which items group together or the differences between sexes and age groups, etc. In this instance there were significant differences between men and women on the first three items (see Figure).

As a double-check on the type of help people are most interested in offering, we also asked them to select their one preferred way of helping—was it through getting to know one handicapped person, being part of a group or helping handicapped people indirectly?

THE THREE DEGREES

Personal

Personal contacts at home with one handicapped person and his or her family were the least favoured option. Overall, only one in six people chose this as their preferred way of helping.

More women than men opted for this; particularly in going to the home of a handicapped person (see above). The 40–59-year-old age group were also more willing for personal contacts than any others, as were people who both knew of local services *and* had met mentally handicapped people in their neighbourhood.

Groups

Items three, four and five involve contacts with handicapped people in groups or in social settings. Just under half the people opted for this type of contact as their main preference. In general, men tended to dominate here, although on the item about joining in social activities, significantly more men (23 per cent) answered 'Prefer not', compared to women (eight per cent). The Group option was most popular with the 20–39-year-old age group and with people who either knew of a local centre or had met handicapped people in their locality, but not both.

Remote

Helping 'indirectly', such as lending a hand at special events, could mean never having to meet and talk with a person who is mentally handicapped. About one-third of people chose this as their preferred way of 'helping'.

These tended to be men, the over 60s and people who did not know of any local services for handicapped people in their area.

These pen pictures of likely volunteers for each style of contact are better regarded as being impressionistic rather than photographic. The clues might help you to target your recruitment drives but, of course, there will be exceptions. There is no prize if you persuade a retired gentleman who has never before met a mentally handicapped person to become a home-teacher for a severely disabled man!

INCENTIVES

What would encourage people to get involved with the mentally handicapped people in their area? Sad to say, this most crucial of topics has been much neglected and not just in the area of disability. There is little to contradict the conclusions of the Aves committee[68] when they wrote, 'Voluntary work at present seems to have an infectious quality and to be something which people catch rather than something which they deliberately seek or which sets out to find them.'

Some of our interviewees had their own opinions:

Time is the major factor determining people's attitude to voluntary work. Woman (20s).

Always the same people who get involved in voluntary work. Man (30s).

A lot of motivation is needed to become involved. Man, late teens.

Too many people involved for selfish reasons. Woman (50s).

Leaving aside personal circumstances which may prevent people from getting involved, are there any incentives which could make voluntary work more attractive? We thought of six 'incentives' (see Figure) and asked our people to say whether each one would *Very much* or *Might* encourage them to get involved, or whether it would *Make no difference*. In addition, we asked them to select from the listing the one item which they considered to be the *Most important* for them.

The results are shown in the Figure and, as you can see, there is nearly a tie for top place.

'Support and back-up from professionals' along with 'helping a handicapped person you know' were nominated by nearly three-quarters of the interviewees.

Conversely, more selfish incentives, such as getting money for expenses or obtaining work experience, were thought important by only a minority of people. Incidentally, the latter was a particular favourite with the under 20s; four out of five saying this would 'Very much' encourage them compared to only half of the 20-39-year-olds, and less than a third of the over 40s. This apart, there were no significant differences among the sub-groups in the sample; all showed a similar pattern in their preferences.

We went on to ask if they would prefer being involved with:

* children (62 per cent of women would, compared to 40 per cent of men). Overall 52 per cent;
* teenagers and adults (30 per cent men would; 18 per cent women). Overall 24 per cent;
* no preference (30 per cent men; 20 per cent women). Overall 24 per cent.

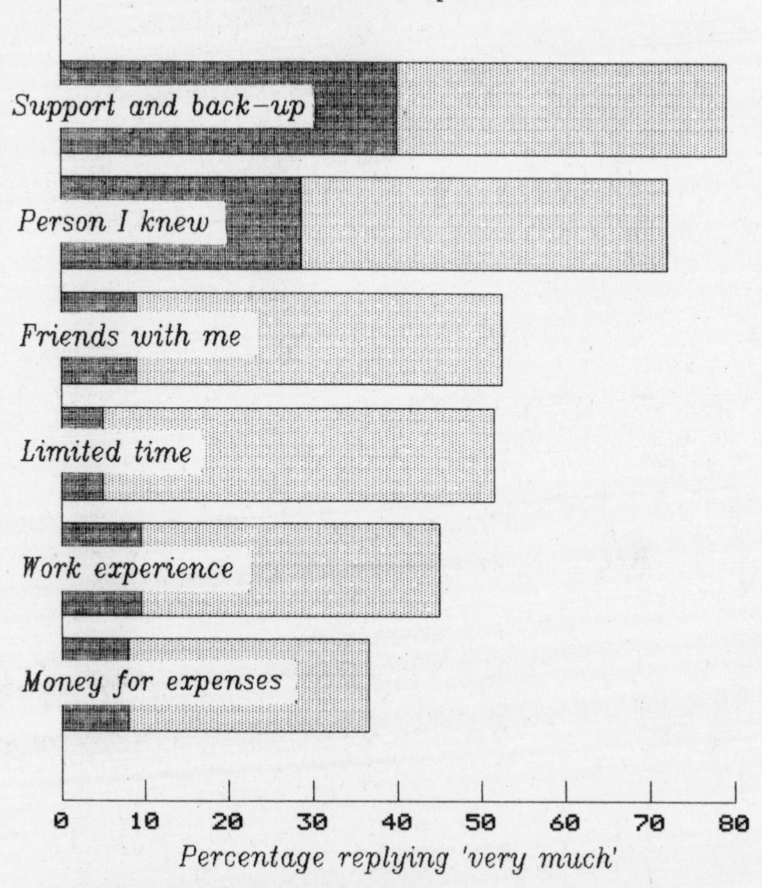

And also whether they would prefer involvement with:

* mildly handicapped people (43 per cent would, especially among 20-39-year-olds);
* severely handicapped people (five per cent would);
* no preference (52 per cent).

Combining both sets of preferences, the following picture emerges:

25 per cent prefer involvement with mildly handicapped children;

13 per cent with mildly handicapped teenagers/adults;
27 per cent with children—mildly or severely handicapped;
11 per cent with teenagers/adults—mildly or severely handicapped;
24 per cent no preferences.

Children and mildly handicapped people probably appear less threatening to the uninitiated.

Rather surprisingly, there were no relationships between all these preferences and people who expressed an interest in doing voluntary work. This suggests that the conditions under which people work are not a crucial factor in determining their interest. Rather, as we have seen, it may have more to do with their past experiences and personal characteristics.

IMPLICATIONS

What, then, have we learnt about the public's perceptions of voluntary work with mentally handicapped people?

First, a significant number of people—around one in four—have had some experience of voluntary work in general. It would appear that the ethos of helping one's neighbours is still alive and kicking—at least in suburban Dublin. The trick might be to encourage more of the volunteers to get involved with mentally handicapped people.

Second, it appears that the men and women most interested in helping people who are mentally handicapped are the ones who have had some contact with these people, either in their local area or through their past voluntary work. Once again, previous contact seems the best preparation for future companionship—and knowing the person whom you are helping is one of the best incentives.

Third, different sorts of contacts appeal to different subgroups within the community. We might be more successful in attracting volunteers if we learned to ask the right people. In our sample, women under forty were the group most interested in helping on a one-to-one level. Which is probably not too surprising when you consider the existing workforce in services for mentally handicapped people, or the people usually involved in charitable work. Special efforts may be required if men are to be encouraged to help at a person-to-person level.

Fourth, volunteers do not want to be left to get on with the job. They expect support and back-up from the professionals. In our recruitment we must spell out precisely how this will happen. Mutual trust and respect between the professional and the volunteer is probably the most crucial element in that much used but ill-defined term 'support'.

Finally, I admit we are still in the dark about the number of people who will actually get involved in helping the mentally handicapped people in their area. Nor shall we know the answer until we offer them a real chance of doing so. However, we can be sure that there will be no absolute percentage to rely on. Rather, the numbers will vary according to the involvement proposed, the conditions under which the scheme will operate and the community to whom the appeal for help is being made. In short, careful planning is essential. But I am convinced that there are sufficient, well-disposed people in all communities for us to start issuing invitations.

10 Who's Your Community?

> There's only one thing I like about holidays, that's looking at trains—and someone to talk to, 'cause you haven't really got people much to talk to.
>
> *Man in his 40s attending Day Centre*

And so we come to the final instalment of the story. If this was a romantic novel, you would now read that they all lived happily ever after. As it is, I have to be content with asserting that they all lived—full stop! Or had it been a detective story, the climax would have been reached and you would now discover 'whodunnit'. In this book, the mystery continues—the end is more a case of who-will-do-it?

I hasten to assure you that this story is not a work of fiction. But there is a sense in which it is like those children's story-books in which you can create different endings for yourself. Let me explain.

You have been given evidence from two Dublin suburbs about their involvement with mentally handicapped people and their perceptions of this disability. You have read people's testimony about their concerns and reactions to closer contact, such as having people with mental handicaps living next door. They have told you about their interest in learning more about this handicap and the ways they might be interested in helping.

Now you are the judge. Do you leave the story at that—a quaint tale of Irish life that would have read better if you had had a plentiful supply of Guinness on hand, but which has little relevance to you and your community? Or has it sparked off even more questions in your mind? Questions like:

* Do the people in my area feel the same about mental handicap?
* How would I go about finding out and, anyway, who *is* my community?
* Even if only a small percentage of local people are interested in becoming more involved, how can their good intentions be translated into actions?
* How can people's misconceptions be corrected and their apprehensions overcome?
* What are the implications for the way services are organised?

If one or more of those questions have crossed your mind as you have read the book, then I shall have achieved what I set out to do. I hope that this last chapter will give you some pointers to show how you might begin to get answers to these questions so that you can write your own ending to the story. It is all a matter of where you are standing—what looks to me like the exit may be your way in.

WHO'S MY COMMUNITY?

It is rather ironical that at a time when great emphasis is placed on the individuality of disabled people—'no two are alike'—we continue to lump together the non-handicapped as an amorphous mass—'the community'. But if our research had taught us no other lesson, this one would stand out:

A COMMUNITY IS A COMMUNITY OF COMMUNITIES

In any geographical area, be it a large suburban housing estate or a closely knit village, there exists not just one community but an amalgam of sub-communities with differing numbers of people in each. Often these sub-groups are defined more by common interests and needs rather than by physical proximity. Moreover, they are rarely firm entities. Their memberships may overlap and people may belong to or identify with more than one grouping.

Mrs Murphy for example, could be grouped with the over-60s, the widows and the bridge players, but another old-age pensioner, Mr O'Brien, is a staunch supporter of the amateur football club and a frequenter of the local pub. He would have little in common with widows and would not be seen dead with the bridge 'set'! Even so, they are life-long neighbours, having reared their families in the same district.

If you think for a minute of the districts or communities which you know well—for instance the one you grew up in—you will appreciate the truth of what I have just described. Every community has its groupings, 'sets' or—in modern parlance—its networks.

It should come as no surprise then, to discover, as we have done, that within the community there is no uniformity of attitudes to disability in general, or to mentally handicapped people in particular. In some instances we have managed to identify the defining characteristics of groups in the community who are most willing to help. At other times, there appears to be no obvious relationship between attitudes and 'group membership', and yet the fact remains that there are discernible differences in people's perceptions and reactions.

A number of implications flow from this analysis:

IN ANY COMMUNITY YOU CAN EXPECT TO FIND A RANGE OF ATTITUDES

Don't tar everyone with the same brush!

EACH NEIGHBOURHOOD HAS UNIQUE GROUPINGS OF PEOPLE

If you don't have 'inside' knowledge of a community through living in it (and most professionals don't) you will need to discover what it is like!

INTEREST GROUPS MAY BE MORE SIGNIFICANT THAN GEOGRAPHICAL COMMUNITIES

It may be more efficient to target your community outreach to certain significant groups in your neighbourhood rather than blitz everyone!

Finally, it goes without saying that the results we have presented for Dubliners may not hold for your community. As far as I am aware, there have been no cross-cultural studies of attitudes to disability. Perhaps you could join with me in making a start?

ASSESSING COMMUNITY ATTITUDES

Learning more about your community's attitudes is not intended as an academic exercise. Rather it should be an opportunity for you to become better informed about the community and to discover likely reactions to topics which are of particular concern to you. In short, you ask the questions to which *you* want answers.

I realise that I could easily have put you off by creating an impression that attitude surveys are very technical and require a great deal of expertise. But if you have survived this far and followed the story up to now, you should have an appreciation of the essentials and an idea of how to set about doing your own piece of research. There is no shortage of excellent texts[69, 70] and invariably you will find someone in your area to give advice. The following tips might make the task easier and you might reread pages 55 to 59 for an overview of the steps involved.

Different types of survey

We opted for the quantitative approach: asking the same questions of large, representative samples of people and quantifying their answers into certain categories. This is the usual opinion poll style of study and is relatively easy to carry out, especially with small numbers of people—less than 100—and a limited number of questions. It is, however, rather time-consuming to conduct when you are dealing with larger numbers of people and/or more questions, and a computer is essential in order to do a full analysis of the results.

There are other approaches. Among the simplest are interviews with 'key' people: for example, in a neighbourhood, talking to the chairperson of the residents' association, the local publican, the postmistress, the school principal, the parish priest or vicar and the police sergeant, would soon give you a picture of community life. And although they might not be able to predict the reactions of locals to mentally handicapped people, they could draw some parallels from previous experiences. This strategy is often commended when a service is contemplating opening a Group Home or Day Centre in an unfamiliar locality.

An extension of this approach is to 'interview' a number of people in depth, possibly as a group. By recording their reactions over a wide range of topics, you should obtain a feeling for the width, if not the intensity, of their concerns. Often this step forms a preliminary to a quantitative study (see p. 97) but assuming the group is not atypical of the community as a whole, it can provide a very good insight into people's attitudes in a short space of time.

Questionnaires—The quantitative approach can also take different forms. You can design a simple questionnaire which people complete by themselves. This can be given out personally to a group of people, e.g. in evening classes at a local college, to workers in a factory canteen. The main points to remember are:

1 keep it short—it should only take five minutes or so to complete, so that it is not a major intrusion on their time;
2 have someone on the spot to deal with queries;
3 get people to fill it in there and then.

Alternatively, the questionnaire could be posted to selected individuals. Unfortunately the reply rate is generally low, even if you enclose a stamped addressed envelope.

Recently telephone surveys have become popular, although there is a risk that people with telephones are not representative of the population as a whole.

Finally, if you do decide to stick with the face-to-face approach we used, the best advice is to keep the questions

to the minimum and always, but always, carry out a pilot run before embarking on the survey proper.

Deciding on questions—The number of questions you could ask of the public is potentially endless. You should begin by listing the information you want to obtain. The next step is to devise questions which will give you this information unambiguously. The more specific you can be in your questions, the more relevant will be your answers. We have given you plenty of examples in this book (see questionnaires in Appendix).

The other factor to bear in mind is that people may tend to give basically the same answer to different questions. This means that if you get the answer to one question you will have a fair idea of how they would respond to others. Hence you can save yourself a lot of effort by selecting key questions. But which are those?

We used a statistical technique called Principal Components analysis[40] to look at the relationships between all the answers which people gave in the door-to-door survey. This isolated four components or factors underlying people's answers and, for each factor, it highlighted the question which best represented that aspect of people's views on mental handicap. The four factors, in order of priority, were:

FACTOR 1: *Contact* All the questions we asked about people's past contact with disabled children or adults clustered together. The 'top' question was the one relating to past contacts with mentally handicapped people, i.e. none, seen around, occasional or regular (see Table).

FACTOR 2: *Information* This factor represents people's interest in getting more information. The question which best tapped this was the one we asked about the scheme in which people in the community are paid to have a mentally handicapped person stay with them. The other was information they would like to have about mental handicap (see p. 128).

FACTOR 3: *Knowledge* Three measures were grouped under this factor—knowledge about the local centre; the type of people who attend and what it means to be mentally handicapped. The best predictor of all were the questions relating to knowledge of the local centre.

FACTOR 4: *Reactions* The final set of answers were those related to people's reactions to meeting mentally handicapped people, and the question which best captured this was reactions to two mentally handicapped people moving in next door.

Two implications follow from this analysis:

a) There are at least four dimensions—or components—to people's attitudes, each relatively independent from the others. In order to have a composite picture, questions should be asked from each area. Moreover, if you were inventing totally new questions, these four dimensions would still hold.

b) The questions which best represent each factor have

Key questions in surveying community attitudes

CONTACT: What contact have you had with mentally handicapped adults?

1 No contact at all
2 Just seen them around
3 Occasional meetings or chats
4 Close regular contact

INTEREST IN INFORMATION: There's talk of a scheme in which people are paid to have a mentally handicapped person stay at their house for a weekend, would you . . . ?

1 Be interested in having a person stay with you
2 Be interested but would want to know more about the scheme first
3 Be interested but it's not possible at present
4 Not interested

KNOWLEDGE: Is there a centre for handicapped people in this neighbourhood?

1 No, there is not
2 Don't know
3 Yes, there is . . . What sort of handicapped people attend the centre? (Open question)

REACTIONS:* If two mentally handicapped adults moved in next door to you, do you think that this would give rise to any problems in the neighbourhood?

1 No it would not
2 Unsure
3 Yes it would . . . Could you say what these might be? (Open question).

* See suggested changes to this question, p. 121.

been highlighted. The pattern of replies to this question is the best—although imperfect—predictor of how people respond to the other questions associated with this factor. Hence if we have answers to the first questions we can risk dispensing with the others. Unfortunately there is no way of knowing in advance whether a new question would be a better predictor. It is worth checking later, though, so that you will know for the next survey.

A note of caution, however; the four factors do not account for all the variations found in people's answers—the total is 56 per cent of which Factor 1 is the main contributor with 24 per cent, and the others 12 per cent, 11 per cent and nine per cent respectively. This is a respectable but incomplete accounting of the differences. The moral is that you cannot have it both ways—if you skimp on the questions you do not get total coverage. Then again, all you may need are indications of likely responses and the four key questions given in the Table would do this.

Interviewing—The texts referenced later[69, 70] contain much useful advice on the mechanics of interviewing which I shall not repeat, except to say that particular attention must be given to avoiding the biases which can inadvertently arise in either the selection of people to interview or their answers to questions. Rather, my tips fall more into the art of interviewing which, now that I think of it, is not too dissimilar from the art of butterfly catching. Ideally you want to catch everyone you approach to take part in the survey without ruffling their feathers. If you have a high number of refusals, your results will not truly represent the community's views.

* *Approach*—The crucial time for eliciting co-operation is the opening seconds, when the approach has been made and the 'target' is weighing up the interviewer. Success usually comes more readily if your interviewers are cheerful, confident and of 'mature' years. It is

easier to say 'No' to people who are diffident, surly and still look like a child! It is vital that all the interviewers are fully briefed and enthusiastic.

* *Choose your time*—Refusals are much more likely if you call at a time when people are busy, e.g. mealtimes. Try to negotiate a time when you might call back, before accepting a 'No'.
* *Introduction*—tell the person who you are—have identification with you—how the survey will be of help and how long you are likely to spend with them.

  Keep the introduction short and succinct. If necessary you may have to include a 'disarming' statement. For example, in the survey about voluntary work (see p. 143–155) we included the sentence 'We're not recruiting volunteers, rather we want people's reactions to voluntary work.'
* *Make a start*—Once people start answering questions, they nearly always keep going. Begin with a simple non-personal question and start as quickly as you can after the introduction of the survey.
* *Encourage*—Throughout the interview maintain a pleasant, encouraging manner and be an attentive listener. Do not be so engrossed in recording answers that you rarely look at the person you are interviewing.

  Equally, be careful that you do not inadvertently bias people's answers. Even small signs of approval/disapproval may influence people's replies. The interviewer's task is to facilitate people in saying what they want to say, rather than getting people to say what the interviewer wants to hear.
* *Further information*—At the end of the interview, be profuse in your thanks. You might explain that each person's replies are added up to give a composite picture and that no individual will be, or can be, identified.

  An offer to supply further information can also be reassuring to interviewees, either in the form of a leaflet or an address or telephone number they can contact. This step is particularly important if there are to be ongoing contacts with the group you interview.

Data analysis

You must have a plan for analysing the data *before* you begin collecting it. This will help to refine the questions you ask and the way you note people's replies. Believe me, the time invested here is rarely wasted.

The next most common mistake is to underestimate the time involved in collating the replies; analysing the data and in writing a report summarising the results. Everyone feels that they are too slow. The use of a computer can be a great help in quantitative surveys, although if you are not already familiar with one, you have the extra chore of learning how to use it.

In sharing your findings with others, figures mean much more than lists of numbers. Incidentally, many computers will draw charts and graphs for you nearly as quickly as print a table of figures.

Finally, a written report which highlights the significant findings should be circulated to those who can act on the information. There is little to be gained in keeping the information 'confidential'.

Carrying out your own survey may not be a realistic proposition for many readers. But this is no excuse for not consulting and listening to people in communities where you live and work. It's not how you do it that is important, so much as the recognition that it must be shown. Be warned: as the American diplomat, Carl Rowan, put it, 'There aren't any embarrassing questions—just embarrassing answers'.

EDUCATING THE COMMUNITY

Discovering the attitudes of a community will not in itself bring about changes for the better. The next step must be to consider ways in which the people of that community can become better informed and more disposed towards mentally handicapped people.

This topic is explored in detail in our book, *Breaking Barriers*[1] which summarises our research findings in this area and describes ready-made educational packages. But the key elements to success can be quickly summarised.

PLANNED PERSONAL CONTACTS

In very many cases, mentally handicapped people are their own best ambassadors. They can win people over. I have recounted many instances in this book in which people who have previously come in contact with mentally handicapped children or adults are much more positive and knowledgeable than their neighbours who have had little or no contact.

The central feature of any educational programme must be an opportunity for the public to meet a disabled peer, in an enjoyable, non-threatening way.

This is more likely to be achieved if:

* They meet in ordinary places rather than in specialist centres. Hence in the short programme on mental handicap which we designed for use with secondary school pupils, a group of trainees from the local centre for mentally handicapped people come to their school. By contrast, the visit by school pupils to the centre is optional.
* They share an activity together rather than relying solely on conversation. For example, in our educational module for shop assistants in city centre stores, they take one or two mentally handicapped people on a tour of the store.
* The people from the community are given some tips in advance of the meeting to allay their fears. For example, seeing a video of people like themselves interacting with mentally handicapped peers.

In our experience, it is best if people's first contact is with individuals with whom they can communicate relatively easily. As their confidence increases, they can be introduced to more severely handicapped people.

TARGET GROUPS

Directing your message to specific groups within the community is not only a more effective use of your energies, but it ensures that you address the issues which are of most concern to the people you want to influence.

Target groups can be as broadly or narrowly defined as you think necessary and can be chosen either because they have—or will have—contact with mentally handicapped people (such as people living in the vicinity of a Group Home), or else they are people whom you want to influence, such as the clergy, police or local politicians. The very act of identifying the significant groups in your area is a major step towards doing something about community education.

It is when we talk in generalities that generally nothing gets done.

MULTI-MEDIA METHODS

Do not put your faith in one approach. Your messages will need to be hammered home in different ways—leaflets, talks, discussions, meetings, video. Particular use should be made of experiential learning techniques so that people have a chance to discover for themselves the truth of what you tell them. It is this point, more than any other, which distinguishes successful attitude change strategies from the well-intentioned failures.

Once-off campaigns are also of limited effectiveness. Community education must be on-going, with the occasional peak, perhaps. Proust summed it up this way, 'The opinions we hold of one another, our relations with friends and kinsfolk, are in no sense permanent, save in appearance, but are as eternally fluid as the sea itself.' A dialogue with the community is needed.

COMMUNITY INVOLVEMENT

Is all this effort worthwhile? Our results should silence the prophets of despair, who proclaim that all attempts to interest the community are doomed to failure. But the pessimists may still remain unconvinced that all the efforts will reap an adequate harvest. Surely the job of caring for handicapped people is best left to professionals rather than risk the vagaries of community participation.

For me, a starting point is to recognise that there are elements of care which professionals will not be able to undertake or, more correctly, for which society will never have the cash to pay them to undertake. Significantly, the 1971 British White Paper on mental handicap services[71] made much the same point in the last of their 15 principles:

Understanding and help from friends and neighbours

and from the community at large, are needed to help the family maintain a social life and to give the handicapped member as nearly a normal life as his handicap permits.

Sad to say, this point never got another mention in the White Paper. If we believe this principle to be true, are we abdicating all responsibility to do anything about it?

Secondly, I am encouraged by what we know about communities to believe that sufficient people are interested in lending a hand and that our efforts to educate and recruit them will be rewarded.

Jodie Walsh's book, *Let's Make Friends*,[2] takes up this theme and gives detailed descriptions of how ordinary men and women can become involved in person-to-person schemes such as respite care, holiday breaks and befriending projects. This information is based on action-research projects carried out in Dublin.

I foresee a new style of voluntary worker, or community helper, as we prefer to call them. Out goes the image of the 'do-gooder', to be replaced with that of a 'benefactor', Robert Edgerton's[72] term for people in the community who had befriended ex-patients of institutions and who were 'very successful at providing affection with respect'.

These appear to be the key features to successful community participation.

PERSON-TO-PERSON COMMITMENT

The first priority is to establish a link with the community helper and an individual person or family, rather than with a centre or a service. Hence his or her loyalty is to the person, not the service.

SUPPORT AND BACK-UP IS READILY AVAILABLE

The helper must have a professional confidant, guide

and supporter. The relationship between the professional and the helper is crucial. They need time to get to know one another and for trust to develop. The flow of information should be two-way and the supporter should take responsibility for maintaining contact rather than leaving it to the helper.

PHASED SELECTION

The need for community helpers can be widely advertised without committing a service to taking on board all those who apply. Complete openness is essential when it comes to describing what the helpers are expected to do—warts and all. They must be under no illusions about what they are letting themselves in for. We find it useful to phase the selection over a number of weeks, so that those who are not keen to continue can bow out gracefully. This period of time also gives the professional staff an opportunity to suss out unsuitable candidates and redirect them elsewhere.

TIME-LIMITED COMMITMENT

People's initial commitment should be limited to a stated period of time or number of sessions. If at the end they do not want to continue, there should be no feeling of anyone having been let down. If they want to continue, a new 'contract' can be entered into, which might redefine the amount of commitment the helper will give. These contracts might also include money payments to cover the helper's expenses, e.g. if looking after a mentally handicapped person at home.

ASSUMED COMPETENCE

From the outset, we emphasise that community helpers can cope with disability. We encourage them to rely on their intuition and to react 'naturally'. This is more easily said than done, but opportunities for helpers to discuss and share these problems with each other are especially helpful. Latterly we have begun to offer more formal training opportunities, but only when a relationship has been established and not as induction training.

The rationale is best summed up in an old Chinese proverb:

> Go to the people, live among them, love them. Start with what you know, build on the best of what they have. When their task is accomplished, their work is done; the people all remark, we have done it ourselves.

A NEW STYLE OF SERVICE

Yet despite all the hopeful ways we have discovered of engaging the community in caring, I am not convinced that this will become a reality unless a radical re-appraisal is made of the way existing services to mentally handicapped people and their families are organised and managed. Michael Bayley[5], for example, had no doubts about the function which professional social services should fulfil:

A partnership of the community at large and the social services is seen as essential to both. It is not a question of the social services plugging the gaps but rather of their working with society to enable society to close the gaps.

The problem is that we have no suitable model for this 'partnership' style of service. Instead we struggle on with outmoded ones.[73] The hospital model has certainly outlived its usefulness for community services, even though the death-rites are far from complete in most countries. Equally, a model based on educational systems or the management structures used in manufacturing or service industries is too constrained to cope with the diversity of needs that arise with mental handicap. The long-term dependency of these clients makes them unique in society and yet the goal of our services is to give them equality of opportunity in community life.

A new style of service is required to meet this paradox. Persevering with an inappropriate service model not only produces an ineffective service to clients but can create intolerable tensions for staff and will certainly reduce their morale and enjoyment for their work. I doubt if financial inducements compensate for these drawbacks.

I cannot pretend to have any answers, although I think it is possible to identify the likely features of a successful community service system. For example:

* It will have devolved rather than centralised decision-making.
* It must be flexible and adaptable to individual needs and changing circumstances rather than bound by rigid routines and job demarcations.
* The service will be based not around buildings but rather on contacts between people in a whole range of settings.
* It will take time to evolve through negotiation. It cannot be imposed.

Two features of present systems must be addressed urgently:

a) The rôle of specialist staff.
b) The decision-making procedures.

The rôle of specialist staff—We need to redefine our specialities around the *functions* which staff fulfil for clients rather than the professional qualifications which they hold.

We would therefore perceive staff as 'family supports' rather than social workers, or 'communication developers' rather than speech therapists. The point being that many so-called 'unqualified' staff—such as the people I have referred to as community helpers—can then take a full rôle within the service. This also means that essential functions within services will not be overlooked, even though staff with a desirable professional qualification are not available.

And when staff with specialist training or experience *are* available, an integral part of their work must involve them in sharing their expertise with others. This could mean that many will not undertake direct responsibility for working with clients. Rather they will have a supervisory function. As others have noted,[74] there is an urgent need to retrain existing professionals to undertake this rôle.

The decision-making procedures—Many of our services are based around the notion of doing things 'to' or 'for' handicapped people with the decisions being taken by service personnel. Such a model was certainly defensible, even if not ideal, when total care was being provided, such as in residential institutions. It is much less appropriate with community-based services, when the care for the handicapped child or adult is shared with the family or community helpers. If they are excluded from decision-making then two dangers may ensue. The families or community helpers become dependent on service personnel and no longer take the initiative in providing for the handicapped person.

Secondly, families and people in the community may well feel powerless to bring about changes in the services available in their area. The consequence is that they may then be offered a service they do not want and refused one which they require.

Shared decision-making requires trust, equal access to information and a willingness to negotiate. It goes without saying that if this does not happen between managers of services and their staff it is unlikely to occur between staff, parents and community helpers.

I suspect that shared decision-making is more easily achieved in small-scale services, in which there is a high degree of personal contact between the servants and the served. I realise that this could mean major discrepancies in the standards attained across services in different areas, but these could be reduced by having some form of monitoring system, for example by the agencies which provide funding.

CHANGING OUTLOOKS

Bill McCord,[75] ended his review of introducing change in human service agencies with these words: 'People cannot be told to accept new paradigms of knowledge which conflict with their existing world view; they must be converted to them.'

Inevitably in this book our focus has been on converting the community, but I wonder if that can realistically proceed without changing the views of significant others. For example, what are we doing to bolster the self-image of disabled people and their view of themselves in society? Paul Hunt,[76] who has a physical disability, expressed it thus:

> If those of us who are disabled live as fully as we can, while being completely conscious of the tragedy of our situation . . . then somehow we can communicate to others an awareness that the value of the human person transcends his social status, attributes and possessions or his lack of them.

How can we ensure that the wishes of mentally handicapped people are respected and that they will have equality of opportunity?

And what are we doing to influence the world view of parents who may be unduly pessimistic? As one Scottish mother put it to Neil Richardson:[77] 'People say, "well society is there to look after him". But Jimmy doesn't belong to society, he belongs to me and his Dad.' Laudable sentiments for the childhood years, but how will Jimmy spend his adulthood? What are we doing to educate parents about new styles of services and to convince them that these are offered as a right and not out of charity?

Most crucially of all, how will specialist professional staff react to the new vision of care by the community, in which their status and influence over decision-making could be much reduced? Precedent suggests that the status quo is desperately hard to change. I fear we shall have to live with tensions between specialist provision and ordinary services; the wisdom of the professional and the intuitions of community helpers and the ever-present balancing of available resources with individual needs. I foresee no Utopia emerging even on a distant horizon.

At its most fundamental, the change that is most needed in everyone's outlook, is in the concept of disability. Marc Gold,[78] for example, eschewed all talk of a person having deficits of intelligence or social competence in his definition of mental retardation. Rather he saw this condition as referring:

> to a level of functioning which requires from society significantly above average training procedures and superior assets in adaptive behaviour, manifested throughout life.

In essence, handicapped people only need more of what we all need.

APPENDIX

Index of Social Competence

Name of Handicapped Person .... Sex ....
Date of Birth .... Aetiology ....
Informant .... Date of Interview ....

Insert in the box the number of the item describing the individual's best level of functioning.

Additional Handicaps

VISION

1 Normal vision (include glasses)
2 Partial sight—problems in mobility
3 Blind for all practical purposes

1 ☐

HEARING

1 Hearing normal (includes deafness in one ear)
2 Partial hearing; hearing aid prescribed
3 Profoundly deaf—only residual hearing

2 ☐

EPILEPSY

1 No fits—no medication
2 Has or had fits; taking medication to control fits; not real problem at present
3 Has or had fits; taking medication to control fits; recurring problem at present

3 ☐

1 + 2 + 3 ☐

Communication Skills

INSTRUCTIONS

1 Can remember to carry out a sequence of instructions, e.g. a shopping list or directions to a place

4 ☐

2 Can remember instructions and carry them out later, e.g. a message from work
3 Follows a simple instruction which can be carried out there and then—'switch on the light'
4 No response when talked to, except to own name

COMMUNICATION

5 ☐

1 Speaks well—intelligible to all; uses appropriate language; able to give accurate information
2 Some difficulty in speaking—lack of clarity or fluency (e.g. may tend to stammer), but language appropriate
3 Difficulty in speech—only intelligible to those who know him/her well
4 No speech—relies on gestures if attempting to communicate

4 + 5 ☐

Self-Care Skills

EATING

6 ☐

1 Feeds self and can manage all activities at table with no problem
2 Feeds self and can manage most activities (e.g. cutting meat), but needs some guidance/help
3 Feeds self competently but needs help in seasoning foods, cutting meat, etc.
4 Needs to be fed or if left alone is a messy feeder

PERSONAL NEEDS

7 ☐

1 Can look after his/her personal needs *completely independently*—cleanliness, toilet, dressing and chooses appropriate clothes
2 Generally looks after personal needs but requires checking and reminding

3 Has to be helped to wash, dress, etc.
4 Dependent on other persons for all personal needs

MOBILITY 8 ☐

1 Able to walk, run and climb stairs with no difficulty
2 Able to walk fair distances (around $1/4$ mile) but finds running and climbing stairs difficult
3 Can walk only short distances; tires easily
4 Unable to walk alone

USE OF HANDS 9 ☐

1 Fully competent use of hands and fingers —can hit nail with hammer, thread needle, use tin-opener
2 Manages most day-to-day activities involving hands—doing up buttons, using knife and fork, tying shoelaces
3 Slow and rather clumsy in using hands but manages some day-to-day activities
4 Only capable of very basic hand skills or not at all

AROUND THE HOUSE 10 ☐

1 Capable of doing most jobs around the house without supervision—makes bed, washes and dries dishes, cleans floor, etc.
2 Attempts most jobs but needs supervision and help to complete the job properly
3 Able to do simple repetitive jobs—setting the table, drying dishes
4 Attempts these simple jobs but cannot do them properly
5 Unable to do any household jobs

PREPARING FOOD 11 ☐

1 Can prepare an adequate variety of meals without supervision

2 Prepares simple hot food without supervision—cooks eggs, warms soups
3 Makes up food which does not require cooking or with which he/she is familar—cereals, teas, sandwiches
4 With supervision, can prepare simple foods
5 Needs all food prepared for him/her

6 + 7 + 8 + 9 + 10 + 11 ☐

Community Skills

READING

12 ☐

1 Can read and follow a series of written instructions, e.g. directions on a packet of food, recipes, etc.
2 Can read and act appropriately to signs giving directions in shops or in the street
3 Recognises own name written down
4 Recognises and picks out around six different labels on tins and boxes of food, e.g. cereals, washing powders
5 Unable to recognise any writing

WRITING

13 ☐

1 Can write short notes, e.g. shopping lists
2 Can write own name and address without help
3 Writes full name without help
4 Writes name and address from copy
5 Unable to write

TIME

14 ☐

1 Regularly uses watch or clock to check timing of activities, e.g. when a friend might call
2 Tells time in hours and minutes, with clock or watch
3 Knows what hour it is by the clock

4 Shows by behaviour that he/she can anticipate some events of the day, e.g. start of TV programme
5 Seems to have no idea of time

MONEY

15 ☐

1 Able to use money responsibly—no difficulty in coping with everyday money transactions; giving right amount and checking change
2 Can select the amount of money appropriate to stated price of article
3 Estimates roughly what different amounts might buy, e.g. if given 50p has some idea of what he/she could get for that
4 Picks out coins by name, e.g. 50p, 10p, etc.
5 No understanding of money

12 + 13 + 14 + 15 ☐

SUMMARY CHART

Shade the appropriate box on the chart according to the totals for each section of the index.

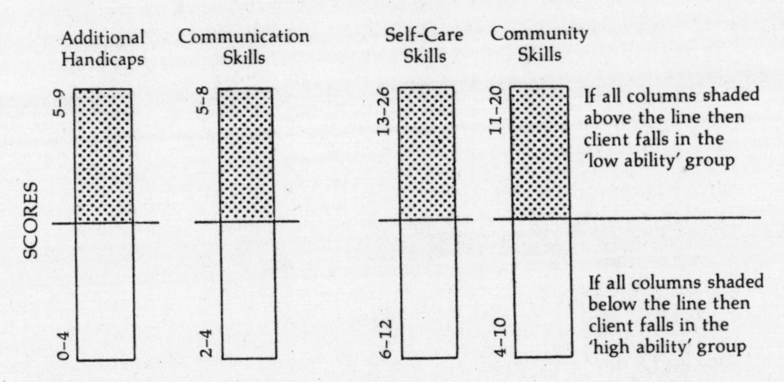

Mixed ability profile—Shaded portions above the line indicate areas in which the person is particularly *weak*.

Questionnaire Used in Door-to-Door Survey

Name . . . . Address . . . .

Interviewer . . . . Date of Interview . . . .

Q.1 *How long have you been living in this neighbourhood?*

[1] Less than a year [2] 1 to 5 yrs [3] 6 to 10 yrs [4] 11 yrs or more

Q.2 *How many families would you know within 15 minutes' walking distance of your house?*

[1] None [2] 1 or 2 [3] 3 to 5 [4] 6 to 15 [5] 16+

How many of these families are related to you?

[1] None [2] 1 or 2 [3] 3 to 5 [4] 6 to 15 [5] 16+

Q.3 *Have you ever asked a neighbour for help?*

[1] Never [2] Sometimes [3] Frequently

Have they ever asked you for help?

[1] Never [2] Sometimes [3] Frequently

Q.4 *What activities are you presently involved in within this area, that is, you could walk to them within 15 minutes?*

Are you involved in	NO	[If YES] – *do you go* *Occasionally*	*Regularly*
Sports clubs in this area	1	2	3
Other clubs in this area (e.g. ICA, bridge)	1	2	3
Bingo in this area	1	2	3
Pubs in this area	1	2	3
Residents' Association in this area	1	2	3
Discos/Dances in this area	1	2	3
Prayer groups in this area	1	2	3
Voluntary work in this area	1	2	3
Political organisations in this area	1	2	3
Night classes in this area	1	2	3
Other 1	1	2	3
2	1	2	3

Q.5 (a) *Is your work within this area, that is, you could walk to it within 15 minutes?*

[1] Yes, within area [2] No, I work outside [3] Housewife [4] Don't work

(b) *Do you work* [5] Student in area [6] Student out of area

[1] Full-time [2] Part-time

Q.6 *Is there a centre for handicapped people in this neighbourhood?*

[1] No, there is not [2] Don't know [3] Yes, there is

(a) Where abouts is it? 1 . . . .

PROBE 'Are there any other centres?' Continue until St Michael's or they say no others

2 . . . . 3 . . . .

(b) What sort of handicapped people attend (St Michael's) Centre (use their wording for the centre)

. . . .

Q.7 *What contact have you ever had with disabled children and adults?*

[1] No contact at all [2] Just seen them around [3] Occasional meetings or chats, e.g. visits to clubs [4] Close regular contact

Q.8 *What do the words 'mental handicap' mean to you?*

. . . .

PROBE (anything else you want to add) . . . .

Q.9 *What contact have you had with mentally handicapped adults?*

[1] No contact at all [2] Just seen them around [3] Occasional meetings [4] Close regular contact

GO TO Q.12

OMIT Q.10 IF THEY DON'T KNOW CENTRE FOR MENTALLY HANDICAPPED

Q.10 *Thinking of people who attend the local centre for the mentally handicapped, have you*

	NO	If YES *was this during . . .* *Past week*	*Past Year*	*Other*
a) seen them on their buses	1	2	3	4
b) seen them walking around the neighbourhood	1	2	3	4
c) have you talked to them outside the centre	1	2	3	4

d) met them inside the centre	1	2	3	4
e) invited any to your house	1	2	3	4
f) other	1	2	3	4

Q.11 CHOOSE IF Q.10 ASKED Thinking now of other mentally handicapped adults whom you have come across, have you any ....

IF Q.10 OMITTED Of the mentally handicapped adults whom you have come across, have you any ....

	NO	If YES *Have you met them during* Past week	*Past year*	*Other*
a) in your close family	1	2	3	4
b) among other relatives	1	2	3	4
c) living in your street	1	2	3	4
d) in the same club as you	1	2	3	4
e) you have done voluntary work with	1	2	3	4
f) you have shared an activity with	1	2	3	4
g) worked with in a service for mentally handicapped	1	2	3	4

Q.12 *In daily life we are often 'forced' to meet people. I would like to get your views on how you would feel if a mentally handicapped adult . . . said hello to you in the street*

1 *Would you prefer they didn't?*
2 *Would it be OK with you?* → *Do you think it's likely to happen?*
3 *Would you encourage it?*

	1	2	3	NO	YES	UNSURE
a) said hello to you in the street	1	2	3	1	2	3
b) sat beside you on bus/train/in café	1	2	3	1	2	3
c) joined in your social activities	1	2	3	1	2	3
d) wanted to become your friend	1	2	3	1	2	3
e) if your best friend (son/daughter) wanted to marry a mentally handicapped adult	1	2	3	1	2	3

Q.13 *If a friend brought a mentally handicapped person whom you had never met before to your house tomorrow, would you . . .* feel embarrassed?

SHOW CARD AND READ

[1] *Definitely Not* [2] *No* [3] *Unsure* [4] *Yes* [5] *Definitely Yes*

Feel embarrassed	1	2	3	4	5	Know what to say	1	2	3	4	5
Find it a good experience	1	2	3	4	5	Know how to react	1	2	3	4	5

I would like to ask you the same questions about your feelings if the friend brought a stranger, who wasn't handicapped to your house, would you . . .

Feel embarrassed	1	2	3	4	5	Know what to say	1	2	3	4	5
Find it a good experience	1	2	3	4	5	Know how to react	1	2	3	4	5

Q.14 *If two mentally handicapped adults moved in next door to you, do you think that this would give rise to any problems in the neighbourhood?*

[1] No it wouldn't [2] Unsure [3] Yes, it would

If YES could you say what these might be?

. . . .

PROBE 'Anything else' . . . .

. . . .

Q.15 *Would you be interested in finding out more about mentally handicapped people?*

	NO	MAYBE	YES
a) Would you watch a programme on TV about them	1	2	3
b) Read a leaflet about them	1	2	3
c) Come to an Open Day in a local centre	1	2	3
d) Support a concert to raise money for them	1	2	3
e) Attend a meeting in the area to learn more about them	1	2	3
f) Go to evening classes on mental handicap	1	2	3

Q.16 *There's talk of a scheme in which people are paid to have a mentally handicapped person stay at their house for a weekend, would you . . .*

[4] Be interested in having a person staying with you

[3] Be interested but would want to know more about the scheme first

[2] Be interested but it's not possible at present [1] Not interested

Q.17 *Finally I would like to ask you some questions about yourself*

Are you [1] *single* or [2] *married*
Have you any children under 12 years [1] No [2] Yes

Did you leave school at [1] 15 years [2] leaving cert [3] went to tertiary level

Which age group would you fall within [1] 18–19 [2] 20–29 [3] 30–39
[4] 40–49 [5] 50–64 [6] 65+

Are you [1] Renting or [2] Buying your house?

Is it done [1] Privately or [2] From the corporation?

Are there any comments you would like to make about the topics we have touched on in this survey?

....

....

....

THANK YOU SHEET

Voluntary Work Questionnaire

Interviewer . . . . Number . . . . . . Date . . . . . .

Area. . . . .

We are interested in people's feelings about voluntary work, especially with mentally handicapped people. You do not have to give your name unless you are interested in getting more information. All replies are treated in confidence.

1 *Do you know of any services or centres for mentally handicapped people, i.e. people who are retarded, in the area where you live?*

No . . . . . . Yes . . . . . .
If YES: Have you been inside the Centre?
No. . . . . . Yes . . . . . .

2 *In your neighbourhood, have you met and talked to any mentally handicapped people?*

Yes . . . . . . No . . . . . .

3 *What contact have you had with mentally handicapped children and adults in general? (Please tick one)*

No contact . . . . . . Just see them around . . . . . .
Met and talked with them . . . . . Regular contact . . . . .

4 a) *Have you ever been involved in any form of voluntary work, not just with mentally handicapped people? (Please tick one)*

No . . . . . Yes in the past . . . . . Yes at present . . . . .

If YES:

b) *What did/does it involve?*

c) *Did/does it involve any contact with mentally handicapped people?*

Yes . . . . . . *No* . . . . . .

5 *In the future, if you had the spare time, what, if anything, would encourage you to get involved with mentally handicapped people in your area?*

Please circle one number per item:

1 = This would VERY MUCH encourage you.
2 = This MIGHT encourage you
3 = This would MAKE NO DIFFERENCE

a)	Money for expenses	1	2	3
b)	Support and backup from professionals	1	2	3
c)	If you were helping a mentally handicapped person you knew	1	2	3
d)	If it was for a limited period of time, say one to two months	1	2	3
e)	If it gave you an opportunity for work experience	1	2	3
f)	If a friend worked on the same scheme as you	1	2	3

6 *From the above list* (items a to f) *please select the option which you consider most important*

Option . . . . . . (Insert letter)

7 a) *If this condition was met, might you prefer being involved with —(Please tick one)*

Mentally handicapped children . . . . . .
Mentally handicapped teenagers . . . . . .
Mentally handicapped adults . . . . . .
Any age group . . . . . .

b) *Would you prefer . . .* (please tick one)

Mildly handicapped people ......
Severely handicapped people ......
No preference ......

8 *There are different ways of helping mentally handicapped people; some are listed below. If, in the future, you had the spare time, please indicate what you might be prepared to do:*

Please circle one number per item
1 = YES, I would do that
2 = MAYBE I would do that
3 = PREFER NOT to do that

a) Would you go to their house? 1 2 3
e.g. to babysit, help with housework, help someone with their reading, etc.
b) Could they come to your home for a visit? 1 2 3
e.g. to give their family a break
c) Could they join you in something you already do? 1 2 3
e.g. shopping, sport, hobby, walks
d) Would you go along with a mentally handicapped person to night classes, cinema, etc? 1 2 3
e) Would you become a helper with a group/club for mentally handicapped people? 1 2 3
f) Would you lend a hand at special events? 1 2 3
e.g. sports days, sales of work, transport them, etc.

9 *Overall, would you prefer* (Please tick one)

a) To get to know one handicapped person ......
b) Be part of a group who are helping ......
c) To help handicapped people indirectly ......

10 *If some of these schemes were available in your area, would you be interested in getting involved?* (Please tick one)

Not possible at present . . . . Perhaps . . . . Yes . . . .

If PERHAPS or YES:
Would you like further details sent to you?

No . . . . . . Yes . . . . . .

Please give name and address

Finally, we would like to have some details about yourself. Are you:
(Please tick)

10 Male . . . . . . Female . . . . . .

11 Age: Less 20 . . . 20–39 . . . 40–59 . . . 60+ . . .

12 Single . . . Married . . .

13 *Are you in full time employment?*
Yes . . . No . . .

14 *In the area where you live do you regularly go to:*
(Please tick)
Clubs . . . . . .
Church . . . . . .
Pubs . . . . . .
Bingo . . . . . .
Community Centre . . . . . .

15 *Would you like to make any comments on the survey?*

THANK YOU VERY MUCH FOR YOUR HELP

References

1 McConkey, R., and McCormack, B. (1983). *Breaking Barriers: Educating people about disability*, London, Souvenir Press.

2 Walsh, J. (1986). *Let's Make Friends*, London, Souvenir Press.

3 Lundström-Roche, F. (1981). *Our Lives*, Dublin, Irish Committee for the International Year of Disabled People.

4 World Health Organisation (1985). *Mental Retardation: Meeting the challenge*, Joint Commission in International Aspects of Mental Retardation, Geneva, WHO.

5 Bayley, M. (1973). *Mental Handicap and Community Care: A study of mentally handicapped people in Sheffield*, London, Routledge and Kegan Paul.

6 Welsh Office (1983). *All Wales strategy for the development of services for mentally handicapped people*, Cardiff.

7 Department of Health and Social Security (1980). *Mental Handicap: Progress, problems and priorities: A review of mental handicap services in England since the 1971 White Paper*, London, HMSO.

8 Department of Health and Social Welfare (1984). *Towards a Full Life: Green paper on services for disabled people*, Dublin, Government Stationery Office.

9 Titmuss, R. (1961). 'Community Care: Fact or fiction?' in R. Titmuss (ed) *Commitment to Welfare*, London, George Allen and Unwin.

10 Wilkin, D. (1979). *Caring for the Mentally Handicapped Child*, London, Croom Helm.

11 Report of the Committee of Enquiry into mental handicap nursing and care (Chairman: Peggy Jay) (1979), London, HMSO.

12 Townsend, P. (1974). 'The political sociology of mental handicap: a case-study of policy failure', in D.M. Boswell and J.M. Wingrove (eds) *The Handicapped Person in the Community*, London, Tavistock.

13 Hogan, M. (1980). 'Normalization and Communitization: Implementation of a regional, community-integrated service system', in R.J. Flynn and K.E. Nitsch (eds) *Normalization, Social Integration and Community Services*, Baltimore, University Park Press.

14 McConkey, R. (1985). *Working with Parents: A practical guide for teachers and therapists*, London, Croom Helm.

15 Mittler, P., and Mittler, H. (1982). *Partnership with Parents*, Stratford, National Council for Special Education.

16 Heron, A., and Myers, M. (1983). *Intellectual Impairment: The battle against handicap*, London, Academic Press.

17 Independent Development Council for people with mental handicap (1982). *Elements of a comprehensive local service for people with mental handicap*, London, King's Fund Centre.

18 Mittler, P. (1979). *People not Patients: Problems and policies in mental handicap*, London, Methuen.

19 Pugh, G. (1981). *Parents as Partners; Intervention schemes and group work with parents of handicapped children*, London, National Children's Bureau.

20 Smithson, L. (1978). *Lesley, the Child We Chose*, London, Mencap.

21 Sherman, S.R., Frenkel, E.R., and Newman, E.S. (1984). 'Foster family care for older persons who are mentally retarded', in *Mental Retardation*, 22, 302–308.

22 Walsh, J. (1983). *Breakaway; A study of short-term family care for children with mental handicap*, Dublin, National Association for the Mentally Handicapped of Ireland.

23 Pathway Employment Service, 169A City Road, Cardiff CF2 3JB.

24 Billis, J. (1981) Project in adult education for mentally handicapped students, London, Mencap: Metropolitan Region.

25 Shennan, V. (1983). *A Home of Their Own*, London, Souvenir Press.

26 Cnaan, R. Adler, I., and Ramot, A. (1986). 'Public reaction to establishment of community residential facilities for mentally retarded persons in Israel', in *American Journal of Mental Deficiency*, 90, 677–685.

27 Kushlick, A., and Blunden, R. (1974). 'The epidemiology of mental subnormality', in A.M. Clarke and A.D.B. Clarke (eds) *Mental Deficiency: The changing outlook (3rd edition)*, London, Methuen.

28 Whelan, E., and Speake, B. (1986). 'Coping and vocational skills of mentally handicapped adults', in *British Journal of Mental Subnormality*, (in press).

29 Kellaher, A. (1985). 'A survey of mentally handicapped adults in County Kildare', in *Impact*, Nov. 5–7.

30 Walsh, J., and Mulcahy, M. (1982). 'Service requirements of adult mentally handicapped persons living in the community', in *Irish Medical Journal*, 75, 1.

31 McConkey, R., and Walsh, J. (1982). 'An index of social competence for use in determining the service needs of mentally handicapped adults', in *Journal of Mental Deficiency Research*, 26, 47–61.

32 Nihara, K., Foster, R., Shellhaas, M., and Leland, H. (1975). *Adaptive behaviour scale for children and adults*, Washington DC, American Association for Mental Deficiency.

33 Williams, R.F. (1986). 'Perceptions of mentally retarded persons', in *Education and Training of the Mentally Retarded*, 21, 13–20.

34 Walsh, J., and Mulcahy, M. (1982). *Residential care requirements of adult mentally handicapped persons living in the community*, Dublin, Medico-Social Research Board.

35 McConkey, R., Walsh, J., and Mulcahy, M. (1981). 'The recreational pursuits of mentally handicapped adults', in *International Journal of Rehabilitation Research*, 4, 493–499.

36 Kastner, L.S., Reppucci, N.D., and Pezzoli, J.J. (1979). 'Assessing community attitudes toward mentally re-

tarded persons', in *American Journal of Mental Deficiency*, 84, 137–144.

37 New Jersey State Department of Health (1981). *New Jersey general public survey*, New Jersey, Division of mental retardation.

38 Gottlieb, J. (1975). 'Public, peer and professional attitudes toward mentally retarded persons', in M. Begab and S. Richardson (eds) *The Mentally Retarded and Society*, Baltimore, University Park Press.

39 Central Statistics Office (1986). *Census of the population of Ireland: 1986, Preliminary Report*, Dublin, Government Stationery Office.

40 Nie, N.H., *et al* (1984). *Statistical Package for the Social Sciences, SPSSX*, New York, McGraw-Hill.

41 Market Research Bureau of Ireland (1981). *Reaction of the general public to physically disabled, and mentally handicapped and ill people*, Dublin, Health Education Bureau.

42 Market and Opinion Research International (1982). *Public attitudes towards the mentally handicapped: Research study conducted for MENCAP* (Available from Mencap National Centre, 123 Golden Lane, London, EC1Y 0RT).

43 Locker, D., Rao, B. and Weddell, J.M. (1981). 'Changing attitudes towards the mentally handicapped: The impact of community care', in *Apex, Journal of British Institute of Mental Handicap*, Vol 9, 92–93, 95, 103.
ibid (1979). 'The community reaction to a hostel for the mentally handicapped', in *Social Science and Medicine*, Vol 13a, 817–821.

44 Groarke, AnnMarie (1986). Community living for persons with mental handicap: A survey of public attitudes. Unpublished report, Galway, Brothers of Charity Services.

45 Okolo, C., and Guskin, S. (1984). 'Community attitudes toward placement of mentally retarded persons', in N.R. Ellis (ed) *International Review of Research in Mental Retardation: Vol 12*, New York Academic Press (Useful review of studies carried out in USA).

46 Roth, R. and Smith, T.E.C. (1983). 'A statewide

assessment of attitudes toward the handicapped and community living programs', in *Education and Training of the Mentally Retarded*, Vol 18, 164–168, (Telephone survey).

47 Sinson, Janice, C. (1985). *Attitudes to Down's Syndrome: An investigation of attitudes to mental handicap in urban and rural Yorkshire,* London Mental Health Foundation (50 mothers of preschoolers interviewed in each location).

48 Gething, L. (1986). 'International Year of Disabled People in Australia: Attitudes and integration', in *Rehabilitation Literature*, 47, 66–70 (focuses on disability in general).

49 Gallup Polls (1981). 'Our image of the disabled and how ready we are to help', in *New Society*, January 1st. 'Has the International Year helped disabled people?' in *New Society*, December 24th (focuses on disability in general).

50 Cheseldine, S., and Jeffree, D.M. (1981). 'Mentally handicapped adolescents: their use of leisure', in *Journal of Mental Deficiency Research*, 25, 49–59.

51 Reiter, S., and Levi, A. (1981). 'Leisure activities of mentally retarded adults', in *American Journal of Mental Deficiency*, 86, 201–203.

52 Mulcahy, M., and Reynolds, A. (1984). *Census of the mental handicap in the Republic of Ireland, 1981*, Dublin, Medico-Social Research Board.

53 Wolfensberger, W., and Kurtz, R. (1974). 'Use of retardation-related diagnostic and descriptive labels by parents of retarded children', in *Journal of Special Education*, 8, 131–142.

54 MacMillan, D.L., Jones, R.L., and Aloia, G.F. (1974). 'The mentally retarded label: A theoretical analysis and review of research', in *American Journal of Mental Deficiency*, 79, 241–261.

55 McConkey, R., McCormack, B., and Naughton, M. (1983). 'A national survey of young people's perceptions of mental handicap', in *Journal of Mental Deficiency Research*, 27, 171–183.

56 McConkey, R., McCormack, B., and Naughton, M. (1984). 'Preparing young people to meet mentally handicapped adults: A controlled study', in *American Journal of Mental Deficiency*, 88, 691–694.
57 Rix, B. (1984). 'How to influence public attitudes', in *Parents' Voice*, Autumn, 4–6.
58 President's Committee on mental retardation (1975). 'Gallup Poll shows attitude on mental retardation improving', in President's Committee on Mental Retardation Message, Washington DC.
59 Webb, N., and Wybrow, R. (1982). *The Gallup Report*, London, Sphere Books.
60 Sitkei, E.G. (1976). Two-year follow-up on mobility rates for a sample of group homes for developmentally disabled persons or after group-home living—what alternatives? Paper presented at 100th meeting of the American Journal of Mental Deficiency, Chicago.
61 Davidson, J.L. (1982). 'Balancing required resources and neighbourhood opposition in community-based treatment center neighborhoods', in *Social Service Review*, 56, 55–71.
62 Sigelman, C.K. (1976). 'A Machiavelli for planners: Community attitudes and selection of a group home site', in *Mental Retardation*, 14, 26–36.
63 Hogan, R. (1986). 'Gaining community support for group homes', in *Community Mental Health Journal*, 22, 117–126.
64 Keller, O.J., and Alper, B.S. (1970). *Halfway Houses: Community-centred correction and treatment*, Lexington: Mass, Heath.
65 Weiner, D., Anderson, R.J., and Nietupski, J. (1982). 'Impact of community-based residential facilities for mentally retarded adults on surrounding property values using a realtor analysis method', in *Education and Training of the Mentally Retarded*, 17, 278–282.
66 Thompson, L. (1986). *Bringing up a Mentally Handicapped Child: It's not all tears*, London, Thorson.
67 Ellis, S.J. (1984). Research on volunteerism: What

needs to be done, Paper presented at AVAS Conference, Blocksburg, VA.

68 Aves, G.M. (1969). *The voluntary Worker in the Social Services*, London, George Allen and Unwin.

69 Honville, G., Jowell, R., and associates (1978). *Survey Research Practice*, London, Heinemann Educational.

70 Kane, E. (1983). *Doing Your Own Research: Basic descriptive research in the social sciences and humanities*, Dublin, Turoe Press (London, Marion Boyars).

71 Department of Health and Social Security (1971). *Better services for the mentally handicapped*, (Cmnd 4683), London, HMSO.

72 Edgerton, R. (1967). *The Cloak of Competence*, Berkeley, University of California Press.

73 Baldwin, S.C. (1983). 'Health care models for people who have mental handicaps', in *Mental Handicap*, 11, 150–152.

74 Roeher, G.A. (1981). 'A balanced approach to personnel preparation and utilization in developed and developing countries', in P. Mittler (ed) *Frontiers of knowledge in mental retardation, Vol 1*, Baltimore, University Park Press.

75 McCord, W.T. (1982). 'From theory to reality: Obstacles to the implementation of the normalization principle in human services', in *Mental Retardation*, 20, 247–253.

76 Hunt, P. (1966). *Stigma: The experience of disability*, London, Geoffrey Chapman.

77 Richardson, J.N. (1979). *Julie?—She's a love. A study of 76 young mentally handicapped children and their families*, Glasgow, Scottish Society for the Mentally Handicapped.

78 Gold, M. (1975). *An alternative definition of mental retardation*, Institute for Child Behaviour and Development, Urbana-Champaign.

Index